�֍ ✤ ✤ ✤ ✤

# BUILDING
# PRODUCTIVE TEAMS

✾ ✾ ✾ ✾ ✾

# Glenn H. Varney

# BUILDING PRODUCTIVE TEAMS

## An Action Guide and Resource Book

Jossey-Bass Publishers

San Francisco    •    Oxford    •    1989

BUILDING PRODUCTIVE TEAMS
*An Action Guide and Resource Book*
by Glenn H. Varney

Copyright © 1989 by: **Jossey-Bass Inc., Publishers**
**350 Sansome Street**
**San Francisco, California 94104**
**&**
**Jossey-Bass Limited**
**Headington Hill Hall**
**Oxford OX3 0BW**

**Library of Congress Cataloging-in-Publication Data**

Varney, Glenn H.
  Building productive teams : an action guide and resource book /
Glenn H. Varney.
      p.      cm. — (The Jossey-Bass management series)
  Includes bibliographical references.
  ISBN 1-55542-180-6
  1. Work groups.   I. Title.   II. Series.
  HD66.V36   1989                                        89-45595
  658.4'02—dc20                                          CIP

Manufactured in the United States of America

The paper in this book meets the guidelines for
permanence and durability of the Committee on
Production Guidelines for Book Longevity of
the Council on Library Resources.


JACKET DESIGN BY WILLI BAUM




FIRST EDITION

*Code 8954*

❀ ❀ ❀ ❀ ❀

# The Jossey-Bass
# Management Series

CONSULTING EDITORS
Human Resources

Leonard Nadler
Zeace Nadler

College Park, Maryland

# Contents

     Teams                                                123

13.  Creating a Productive Team Culture                   128

14.  Taking Charge of Team Productivity                   134


     Appendix: Additional Resources on Effective
     Team Management                                      139

     References                                           143

     Index                                                145

✿ ✿ ✿ ✿ ✿

# Tables, Figures, and Exhibits

## Tables

## Figures

## Exhibits

✽ ✽ ✽ ✽ ✽

# Preface

A little over a decade ago, American businesses realized that foreign companies had successfully captured large segments of American markets. This sudden and somewhat rude awakening prompted much study of how the competition had accomplished this, and so the parade of American managers to Europe and the Far East began.

What the Americans found in some of the most productive organizations (such as Volvo, Sony, and Phillips), aside from an astute ability to copy and improve on excellent technology, was the unusual loyalty and dedication of the workers. When the Americans wondered how this could be, they found the answer in the efficient use of teams and the involvement of the employee in his or her work. Armed with this information, American management began a concentrated effort to develop a team concept and especially to *build productive teams* in their organizations.

## Audience

Although managers in general and American managers in particular are well versed in the financial, production, marketing, information systems, and quantitative aspects of their work, they tend to be inadequately prepared to manage the way people work together. The realizations that jobs within organizations have become more interdependent and that improving teamwork positively influences productivity have stimulated an intense drive to learn more about how to manage teamwork.

*Building Productive Teams* is focused primarily on this need: it provides managers with the knowledge, skill, and insight necessary to manage teamwork and thereby improve productivity. Whereas other books on this subject offer a potpourri of techniques ranging from methods of assessing values to ways of helping people listen to each other, this book gives managers firsthand, applicable information on how to establish and systematically build a team by learning how to fine-tune the factors that affect its work. For example, I approach the task of building a productive team from an analytical viewpoint; you can not fix problems that a team has unless you thoroughly understand what is going on in the team. As a result, there are four chapters on how to take your team apart, analyze it, and put it back together again.

Although I use the generic term *manager* to define the audience for this book, *Building Productive Teams* is a valuable source of information for everyone who works with other people. In our society, many tasks are accomplished by groups of people solving problems together, so it is almost impossible to find situations in which teamwork is not required. The content of this book has been tested and used by large and small U.S. organizations ranging from Silicon Valley companies to hospitals and schools. The ideas and insights presented here can be integrated into day-to-day management by all people who are responsible for teams, including chief executive officers, teachers, university administrators, line managers, project managers, trainers, consultants, and many others. In short, this book can help almost anyone learn more about working with teams and improving results through teamwork.

### Overview of the Contents

The book is organized to take the reader from basic questions about teamwork to the specific problems inherent in building a productive team. Chapter One introduces a model for studying and understanding teams; then Chapters Two through Nine discuss the model in detail, including recognizing symptoms of unproductive teams, analyzing teams, planning for team improvement, clarifying team member roles and goals, managing team member relations, designing decision-making and problem-solving procedures, and identifying the role of leadership in high-performing teams. Chapter Ten examines a detailed example to illustrate how team problems may be resolved, while Chapter Eleven discusses how to build a strong foundation when new teams are formed, thereby ensuring a high level of productivity. Because many organizations are training managers in team management, Chapter Twelve provides some proven ways to help managers learn the necessary skills. Chapter Thirteen looks at how a healthy and productive team culture is created and suggests ways managers can achieve this. Chapter Fourteen stimulates the reader to take action and use the content of this book by offering a number of ways to take the initiative in improving team productivity.

## Acknowledgments

There are several people whose contributions helped to create this book, and they deserve recognition. They are Janice McKnight, Greg Anderson, Leonard and Zeace Nadler, and a very persistent and dedicated editor, Steve Piersanti.

*Bowling Green, Ohio*                    Glenn H. Varney
*August 1989*

# The Author

Glenn H. Varney is professor of management and director of the master in organization development program at Bowling Green State University. He is also president of Management Advisory Associates Incorporated, a management consulting firm specializing in improving organization effectiveness. He received both his B.S. degree (1949) in business administration and his M.B.A. degree (1951) from Ohio State University, and his Ph.D. degree (1971) from Case Western Reserve University in organization behavior.

Varney's research and publishing interests have centered on ways to improve organizational performance, with special interest in improving team productivity. He has developed methodologies for evaluating team effectiveness and published numerous articles on the subject. His books include *Management by Objectives* (1972), *Organization Development Approach to Management Development* (1976), *Organization Development for Managers* (1977), *Teambuilding: A Self-Directed Approach to Improving Work Teams* (1985), *Goal-Driven Management* (1987), and *Improving Productivity by Objectives* (forthcoming).

✿ ✿ ✿ ✿ ✿

# BUILDING
# PRODUCTIVE TEAMS

## 1

# Dynamics of
# Successful Teamwork

The improvement of team productivity is certainly one of the most challenging tasks that today's organization encounters. A team-oriented approach to management is both dynamic and progressive, yielding such benefits as increased performance, improved quality, higher levels of job satisfaction, and the release and utilization of the powerful creative forces within each organization.

In an effort to turn around recent misfortunes, a major American corporation decided to locate a plant in a small Indiana town, hoping that this move to a rural community with a strong work ethic might alleviate many of the problems experienced in the corporation's older plants. The corporation thought that a small-town atmosphere would ensure conditions conducive to high levels of productivity. After the plant began operation, productivity did increase, and a strong and dedicated employee team began to take shape.

The young people of the town who took jobs with this company had been encouraged to help the company succeed, and eventually the entire community adopted a positive attitude toward the company. Wisely, the company accurately diagnosed the factors that contributed to the success it was experiencing. It had appointed a plant manager who shared the values of the people being hired. The manager was participative and believed that people working together could solve problems and accomplish the organization's objectives. Employees helped set their own standards of performance for production and were encouraged

1

to take an active role in determining how the plant, and particularly their own work teams, would be managed. In short, the company had created a team-oriented culture that fit the community, and it was thus able to develop a highly productive organization.

Many communities favor a collaborative or team-oriented approach to work, as opposed to the more traditional and directive styles of managing, and this preference for group orientation has been spreading across the United States during the past several decades. Heeding the continuing trend while aiming to increase both productivity and employee satisfaction, many organizations are experimenting with new forms of team management.

Throughout the world, a battle is being waged that centers on both increased productivity and the quality of products with worldwide distribution. Although Japanese companies are leading the charge, American organizations are also seeking new ways to improve quality while increasing productivity to beat the competition. The value of the quality-circle concept, which was first appreciated in Japan, is finally being accepted in the United States, where the concept, which emphasizes the importance of releasing the untapped skills and resources of the people within an organization, originated.

Numerous organizations have failed because they did not consider the character of their work force. Our society has moved from the formalistic to the collaborative. Today, the people who work in organizations demand a chance to be involved, and they expect to have their talents and skills utilized effectively; they are also willing to participate in activities that will make the organization perform more effectively. Because it has become generally accepted that creativity and innovation are traits widely distributed through the population, managers must be able to discover and put to use these resources within their teams. Once creative forces are unleashed within an organization, the potential for positive results is greatly enhanced.

Although many American managers receive powerful rewards for making decisions on their own, the results of extensive research (Likert, 1961; McGregor, 1985; Argyris, 1971; Lorsch and Lawrence, 1972; Jewell and Reitz, 1981) indicate that collective decision making is a more productive process than individual decision making. The overall quality of decisions and the general success rate of an organization increase substantially when decisions are reached through collective or consensus processes. When many sets of eyes are brought in to examine a thing, every angle is usually seen. With the current widespread application of the participative approach, this style is being taught in business schools and universities throughout the United States and across the world. Whenever a young manager seeks employment, the interview usually includes the following question: "How much experience have you had with team management?" No matter what degree of experience a manager has had, a further study of the workings of team management is both informative and rewarding, as the characteristics of teams and teamwork are never static.

General Motors conducted a major experiment in team management during the late 1960s and discovered that a team-based assembly operation established in tandem with a production-line operation resulted in a much higher quality of product and a higher level of job satisfaction without an increase in the time required to produce a car. The company also learned that while some people are oriented to team-based assembly, others are not. The older the team members, the more oriented they were to traditional forms of production-line management, and the more difficulty they experienced working in team formats; the younger the team members, the more oriented they were to collaborative values, and the easier it was for them to work in a team format.

Although the importance of teamwork should be obvious, there are far too many managers who overlook its significance for one reason or another. Ignoring the mechanics of teamwork will undoubtedly lead to trouble, and any attempt to manage a group of individuals without an understanding of the functions of successful teamwork is about as likely to succeed as a novice's attempt to operate a sophisticated home computer by first throwing away the instructions. Managers must recognize that what they are able to accomplish as managers will be the direct result of their ability to manage teamwork.

In managing teamwork, the aim should be to manage in a style that brings into action the following aspects of a team:

(1) Productivity goals are accomplished by the individual team members, and therefore the collective goals of the team are also achieved. (2) The members of the team develop high levels of satisfaction and commitment, and they are energized to accomplish the things that need to be done. (3) The abilities, skills, talents, and resources of team members are used to the fullest. When these conditions are present, the quality of the product or service increases.

In an organization in West Virginia, the unchecked impulse of one individual for grandstanding turned out to be highly unproductive, as well as a bit humiliating to both himself and his team. The plant had purchased two cleaning machines driven by internal combustion engines. Without exception, the rank and file and the supervisory group were delighted with this equipment, since it meant a cleaner plant. However, when it came time to make use of the new machines, no gasoline could be found. In a meeting with the plant management staff, the superintendent and supervisors threw up their hands and said, "It's not our responsibility." The purchasing agent said that it was not his responsibility; he could act only when he received a purchase order. The maintenance manager, when asked why he had not submitted a purchase order, complained that nobody had given him authorization to do so. While this discussion continued, the personnel manager was developing his own approach to solving this rather simple problem. He jumped out of his chair, ran into the parking lot, took the company car, and disappeared. Approximately five minutes later, he came back with the siren blowing on the company car and a can of gasoline in his hand. He brought the can into the meeting, where by this time the managers were discussing other topics, and set it in the middle of the table. His purpose was to embarrass and degrade the group of people who were passing the buck; he did this quite successfully. This example illustrates how disregarding the required ingredients of successful teamwork results in buck passing and antagonisms that can lead to rather ugly and counterproductive situations.

The significance of teamwork has not materialized out of thin air (Mayo, 1945; McGregor, 1985). Numerous socioeconomic influences within our culture and our organizations have necessitated an intensive investigation into the fundamental components that enable a group of individuals to work together effectively. With the changing face of our society, old-style approaches to managing are often no longer feasible. In light of the tremendous leaps in technology and the advances in the overall capacity to control most operations within an organization, there is no reason that the manager's ability to release the on-tap potential of team members should not keep pace with such strides being made in other fields. The only major obstacle standing in the way of successful teamwork is a manager's refusal to discard obsolete management approaches. It is helpful to regard the task of team management as a set of skills in managing that are different from the more traditional management skills. The important thing to understand is the basic principles and practical applications of the team-management approach; once these basics are understood, their value rapidly becomes apparent.

As managers begin to examine their teamwork responsibilities, they often are confronted with numerous obstacles that seem to block the path to building successful teams. Many of these obstacles are simply the typical problems of resistance that are encountered whenever real change is suggested; some are carry-over results of old-style American management or societal assumptions about an individual's place in a group. In America, such a high premium has been placed on individual achievement that sometimes the power of the individual is promoted at the expense of teamwork. The headlines read, "Ruth's Homer Wins World Series," as if the rest of the Yankees had never left the bench. Though teamwork is always what gets the job done, it is the "star" who is glorified. As a result, managers have been taught to be rapid decision makers, oriented toward action for action's sake, and overly competitive. When managers are presented with the value of becoming a better team manager, a common response is, "What's in it for me? How can I be both competitive and a team leader?" This is like asking, "How can I drive a car and know where I'm going at the same time?" The very nature of a team is to be competitive—but as a group in competition with other groups, not as a set of individuals struggling against each other. When individuals chase after solitary and isolated objectives, the team effort is put in jeopardy. For effective teamwork, the success of the team must supersede individual success: that is, individuals win or lose as a team.

Along similar lines, many American managers are reluctant to encourage the participation of other members in the decision-making process because they fear that such a sharing of responsibility will be interpreted by higher-ups as a sign of weakness, and that consequently their value to the organization will be diminished. But in point of fact, results, not self-perception, are what determine a manager's worth to an organization.

Both time and patience are required to implement a plan of teamwork. It is an undisguised fact that when time is taken on the front end of work, much less time is wasted in troubleshooting and fire fighting once the work is in progress. A characteristic American management approach is to rush headlong into a project and then try to solve problems as they arise, costly problems that should have been anticipated and dealt with in the planning stages of the project. Clearly, since it takes time to successfully implement teamwork, it will also take time before obvious payoffs begin to appear. The fruits of efficient teamwork are not immediate: no fireworks and brass bands. Payoffs are manifested in subtle ways, comprehensive improvements that affect overall performance, surging out like a potent fertilizer through the limbs of an organization. There are two basic dividends that a manager can count on when implementing teamwork: the confidence that results will improve and the satisfaction of fostering the increased productivity of the team.

However small the effort may at first appear, managers can learn to apply team management practices that will benefit the organization and its members, as well as the managers themselves. Sometimes, an individual manager attempts to positively alter an organization to provide a better place to work and initiate a more productive environment. One such manager worked in a small plant in Ohio. He set out to develop a new vision for his plant, and he did this collaboratively with his employees so that they would feel involved in the effort. Groups of employees throughout the plant were organized to look for ways to improve operations as well as ways to improve the lives of those who worked there. The results led to a major change in the technical operation, the restructuring and expanding of jobs, the sharing in the profits of the plant, and a group of people who felt more committed and more involved in the organization than ever before. The plant became an operating success.

Admittedly, team management aspects are more intangible than finances, scrap rate, and other operational aspects of the job. Nonetheless, managerial team building plays a centrally critical role in advancing productivity. Although it is on the "soft" side of managing, team management is on an equal or higher plane with the "hard" side of managing. An effective and productive team does not arise by accident. Such teams are the direct result of a manager attending to four things. First, the development of team management skills and the commitment to continuous learning are crucial elements. Most of what we know about building productive teams is not taught at universities, as are such management aspects as finance, marketing, production, and so forth. Many team management skills must be learned independently. Second, a manager must recognize that teams are living entities, that they come to life, grow, develop, mature, and eventually die. Managers must recognize the stage at which a team is operating. Creating a productive team demands subtly different skills from those required to successfully manage a team in its mature stage. (For example, when a major oil company formed a new geology team, the young members who were chosen had not worked together before, and thus there were no established relationships or practices to encumber the team and the group could set out to establish a productive team culture. This team, because it thought out how it wanted to work, went on to be a strong and productive group.) Third, given that there are substantial differences between productive and unproductive teams, managers must understand what makes up a productive team. Successful teams embrace the following concepts:

- Team member roles are clear to each person, as well as to others on the team, and individuals are committed to their jobs and accept and support the roles of others.
- Individuals have goals (performance measures) that they have agreed to. The sum of individual goals adds up to the team goals.

- Structure, practices, policies, and systems are understood and agreed to by all team members.
- Working relations are seen as an essential part of an effective team; therefore, they are discussed, and interpersonal problems are solved and not left to fester.

Finally, knowing what constitutes effective teamwork is only part of what a manager must understand; a manager must also know how to diagnose what is going on in the team. Casual observation is not enough. Managers must develop diagnostic and problem-solving skills in order to build teams and correct learning problems. Improperly defining problems can lead only to incorrect solutions.

The model shown in Figure 1 (Rubin, Fry, and Plovich, 1978) illustrates how the elements of teamwork can successfully

**Figure 1. How a Productive Team Works.**

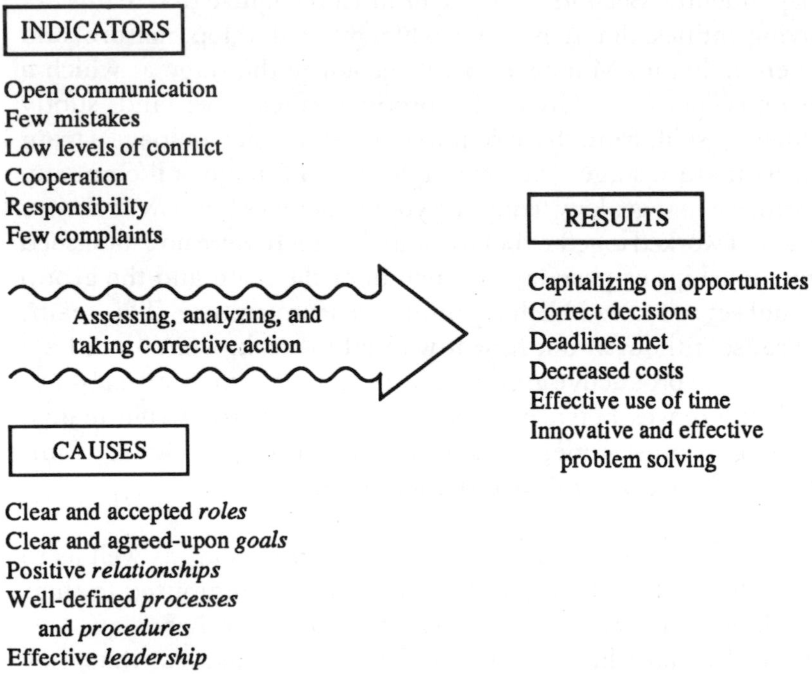

INDICATORS

Open communication
Few mistakes
Low levels of conflict
Cooperation
Responsibility
Few complaints

Assessing, analyzing, and
taking corrective action

CAUSES

Clear and accepted *roles*
Clear and agreed-upon *goals*
Positive *relationships*
Well-defined *processes*
    and *procedures*
Effective *leadership*

RESULTS

Capitalizing on opportunities
Correct decisions
Deadlines met
Decreased costs
Effective use of time
Innovative and effective
    problem solving

mesh if properly managed. Results (productivity)—innovation, meeting deadlines, cutting costs, making correct decisions, and so on—are a direct consequence of how people work together in teams. When the key factors of roles, clarification, agreed-upon goals, correct processes and procedures, effective interpersonal relationships, and good leadership are all in place and working well, the team is able to produce the expected results. When they are not, results suffer. Often, teams slip into patterns and habits that hinder their productiveness. Managers need to recognize when this is happening and take appropriate corrective action. The content of this book is organized around the model displayed in Figure 1. The next eight chapters discuss the model in detail, presenting a logical, step-by-step approach to improving team productivity.

# ❧ 2 ❧

# Recognizing
# Unproductive Teams

The symptoms of an unproductive team are often elusive and scattered, remaining invisible to those who work most closely with the team. As with the proverbial iceberg, what can be observed above the surface is only a fraction of the real calamity. Managers frequently misjudge a problem situation because they fail to comprehend the magnitude of factors that lurk beneath the surface.

In one health care organization, the president held a tight rein on the flow of communication among members of the executive committee; he communicated to all members individually, and they reported back to him one at a time. But one particular channel of communication had gone unnoticed by him. In committee meetings, whenever the treasurer had something to say to the controller, he would direct his question or comment to the president and ask that the president communicate it to the controller; he never made eye contact with the controller or spoke directly to him. The controller communicated with the treasurer in the same unusual fashion. It was not until an outside consultant was sitting in on a staff meeting that this peculiar form of communication was noted and called to the attention of the president and the explanation that had been concealed beneath the surface finally emerged: many years before, there had been a bitter conflict between the treasurer and the controller that led to a permanent falling out, with the result that neither would speak to the other except through the president. Unfortunately, the symptoms of poor teamwork can sometimes be accepted as part of a routine and thus remain unnoticed by those who are closest to the problem.

For a manager to improve teamwork, and hence team productivity, he or she must develop a high level of sensitivity to the telltale signs of unproductive teamwork. An extensive degree of awareness is required to identify and then correct actual or potential problems. All team problems have a cause-and-effect relationship, and the aspect of the problem that can be observed on the surface is very rarely its cause. The significance of symptoms in terms of their effect on teamwork and productivity is often disregarded. The importance of tracking a symptom, searching beneath it, and uncovering its cause must be given more attention by managers who desire an increase in team effectiveness.

## Categories of Symptoms

*Verbal and Nonverbal Communications.* Frequently, the spoken word is manipulated in a manner that conceals feelings and hides intent. Nonverbal communication often discloses what the spoken word has not revealed; there is a message in the frown that accompanies a presentation, a message in the strong, confident clasping of hands at the close of a meeting. The complexity of communication channels can result in awkward situations.

Just before Christmas, a meeting at one company was about to adjourn when the chairperson said, "We will see you after Christmas. I hope you all have a pleasant holiday"; a member of the group followed this remark by saying, "I hope that we will see you at five o'clock tonight." He was referring to a Christmas party at another member's home to which some members of the group had not been invited. After he had made another comment about meeting at five, the person who was hosting the party gave him a stern look, and it finally dawned on him that he had created an embarrassing situation for the host. In this case, a stern look communicated a message without words.

Nonverbal communication is quite common and can convey numerous positive or negative messages. When managers are observing what transpires in groups, they need to pay close attention to all nonverbal signals. Nonverbal cues give substantive clues to the problems that a team may be experiencing. For example, when a member of a team suddenly pushes his or her chair back from the table and stops talking, a strong signal has been sent indicating that this person is pulling out of the conversation and will no longer participate.

*Direct and Indirect Symptoms.* It is often difficult to identify what exactly has caused a symptom. For instance, the reasons that people fail to attend meetings are numerous and varied (illness, another task that has priority, a distaste for the chair or other members of the team, and so forth), and each particular reason could reveal another set of causes. However, a decrease in attendance at meetings could be an indirect symptom of a real problem within the team, and so it should not be dismissed lightly. Other types of indirect symptoms include productivity declines, decreases or increases in verbal activity within the team setting, reports not being prepared on time, and so forth. These types of indirect indicators should be examined to determine the root cause behind each symptom.

Direct symptoms are far more obvious. When, during a meeting, someone blurts out, ''I think that report is totally inaccurate,'' there can be no question as to what the intended message is or to whom it is directed. Open conflict among team members is another patent symptom; although the precise cause behind such a symptom must be uncovered, there can be no doubt that the fighting involves some issue surrounding work.

*Individual and Group Behavior.* Instead of directly expressing an opinion about a particular person or subject, people often attempt to conceal their views within what is presented as a group statement; for example, ''I think I speak for the entire group when I say. . . .'' A person who makes such a statement has probably communicated with several other members of the group to gain reinforcement for his or her already formed opinion before putting forth that opinion in the guise of a group statement.

In one hospital, a group of nurses signed a petition protesting the shifting of work schedules and sent it to the administrator of the hospital, with copies to the director of nursing and the associate administrator responsible for the nursing staff. The nurses were collectively expressing an opinion that there was a problem with the altered working hours. Usually, the catalyst behind a group protest is one individual who strongly influences other members of the group, but individuals will also take strong stands on their own. A person who feels extremely upset will register a complaint or protest about the offending activity or person within the team setting; in highly volatile situations, the person might threaten to quit or to take some other rash action. In any event, such symptoms are clear, and their origins are easy to trace.

Understanding symptoms is the starting point in the process of uncovering the underlying malady. A manager's task is similar to that of the physician; a headache, like a team problem, could have any number of causes, but alleviating a specific headache does not necessarily do anything to remedy its cause. As with the physician, the manager's job is to get behind the symptoms and root out their cause. It is also the responsibility of the physician or manager to anticipate what will occur if the symptoms continue. For example, if kidney trouble is the underlying, but as yet undiscovered, cause of a backache, and if the backache persists, the eventual outcome could be kidney failure. If at first no apparent cause can be found to explain the symptoms, the physician or manager must keep digging until the true cause is unearthed. A word of caution is needed at this point. It is hard for most managers to take an objective role in looking at problems of a team of which they are a part. Diagnosing a team's problems requires that the manager step back from the role of participant and take an unbiased look at how the team is functioning.

To get beneath a symptom, it is necessary to go back to the way in which the team was organized and how it was intended to function. The trick is to uncover the various potential causes that are contributing to the observed symptoms. In some cases, the potential cause appears obvious. It is easy to claim that conflict is caused by poor relationships among members, but one must go further than this to lay bare the true root of a problem: what particular encounters and disagreements between members are causing the conflicts. Communication breakdowns have two probable causes: a failure to clearly define goals and roles and a failure to reach an agreement between members on how they are going to share information.

At a recent meeting of members of a management information service department, the manager asked why a particular project was not on schedule. One of the members responsible for completing the project replied, ''I don't have the information that I need from Bill.'' Bill immediately took exception to this, saying, ''I don't have the necessary information to get this job done so that I can pass it on to Bob as he needs it.'' This was an obvious symptom involving two people who were miscommunicating and passing the buck. When this symptom was investigated, it was discovered that, although the timetable of the goal was clearly defined, the responsibility for obtaining a certain piece of necessary information had been left up in the air. Each member assumed that the other was responsible for obtaining the key information. The solution to this problem was simply to delegate the responsibility to specific people who were involved and get on with the job.

Managers need to understand what unattended symptoms can lead to and for how long they have gone on undetected. Symptoms are an aspect of the cause-and-effect relationship that one can get a handle on. Manifest symptoms of a team problem must be tracked down to their root causes, but it is extremely important to realize that, in improving teamwork, cause-and-effect relationships are complicated and often difficult to establish. A single cause can lead to a variety of effects, and a single symptom can reflect an assortment of causes.

## Typical Symptoms and Their Possible Meanings

Berelson and Steiner (1964) provide a number of examples of typical symptoms and their possible meanings to facilitate an awareness and understanding of the symptoms of poor teamwork.

*Cautious or Guarded Communication.* When people fear some form of punishment, ridicule, or negative reaction, they may either say nothing or be guarded in what they do say. They may utilize defensive wordings such as "perhaps," "possibility," "this is only hypothetical," and so forth.

*Formal or Structural Communication.* When a person chooses to formalize a communication (for example, put it in the form of a letter) that could otherwise have been delivered personally, this suggests a concern for how the receiver will treat the information. Another sign of such concern is sending copies to a number of other people. Formal communication can also be detected in the way a letter is structured. Legal terminology and explicit directions are further indications of highly formal communication. Formal communication responses include statements such as "Put it in writing."

*Lack of Disagreement.* When there is little or no disagreement among a group of people working together, it is quite possible that the members of the group, for one reason or another, are unwilling to share their true feelings and ideas. When there are healthy differences, people will make statements such as "I have a thought on this matter" or "Here's how I see it."

*Failure to Share Information.* Members of a team often have valuable experience involving a particular point of discussion; in some cases, they may even know how to solve the problem. When such people hold back information and do not share their expertise with others, the destructiveness of poor teamwork is in motion. In healthy situations, team members will say things like "I have some information that may help you" or "My files are open to you."

*Reliance on Criticism.* Criticism, particularly when delivered in the presence of others, is a form of punishment that will inhibit people from sharing ideas and making suggestions. Criticism is usually employed when people are not working well together. It is important that a manager refrain from irresponsibly making overcritical comments such as the following: "Only a complete idiot would do what you did." "If you can't come up with better ideas than that, you'd better just keep quiet."

"If you had a brain, you'd be dangerous." "What! Another one of Joe's off-the-wall ideas?"

*Lack of Individual Feedback.* When teams are working well, members receive frequent, constructive, and specific feedback, given in a positive way: "Let's talk about the missing data and see if we can help Sally get the information she needs to complete the project." In a poor team, there is little or no feedback, and what there is is usually negative: "You messed it up again, Pete. When are you ever going to get it straight?"

*Poor Meetings.* Meetings serve as an excellent barometer for measuring teamwork. It is likely that a counterproductive team is at work if, when a group of managers meets to discuss a problem, any of the following symptoms are present:

- A nonexistent or unclear agenda.
- General boredom or lack of enthusiastic participation.
- Long, poorly structured meetings.
- A failure to reach decisions.
- One or two people dominating all discussions.
- People being put down and stymied.

It is not hard to detect poor meetings; just listen to what people say as they walk out: "I'm glad that's over!" "We accomplished nothing." "What a mess."

*Unclear Goals.* When a member of an effective team is asked what the team's objectives are, he or she should be able to describe exactly how the team's efforts fit into the overall goal of the organization. When asked about goals, team members should be able to recite their own as well as their team's objectives.

*Low Commitment.* When goals are routinely dictated to team members, there will be a low level of commitment to achieving those goals. It is not uncommon for people to make statements such as "These are not my goals" or "I had nothing to do with it."

*Unrealistic Goals.* Poor teams draft goals that most members of the team feel have been set unrealistically high and are therefore unattainable.

*Conflict Within the Team.* If there is destructive conflict among team members, it will lead to a suspicious and combative environment. Effective teams recognize that a certain amount of conflict is inevitable, but they also know that conflict can be managed to the benefit of individual members and the efforts of the team. Conflict does not usually surface verbally unless it is at a pressure peak. Nonverbal signals must be observed.

*Failure to Utilize Team Members' Talents.* Ineffective teams are often unaware of the diversity and different levels of skills of team members, and thus the talents and skills available to the team are not fully used. In such a situation, members express their attitudes through telltale comments: ''I've been there before.'' ''It's their loss, not mine.'' ''They'll have to learn the hard way.''

*Performance Evaluation Based on Personal Opinion.* When team members know their jobs and goals, they should be evaluated on the basis of concrete results. In poor teams, the opposite is true; performance reviews are often based on subjective opinions, personal views, and other intangible elements. When evaluation is subjective, individuals will rightly feel cheated.

*Competition Among Team Members.* When team members are openly competing with each other, they hold back information, discredit others' ideas, and attempt to maneuver themselves into favorable positions of power or influence. Such competitive people often take credit for the work of others. Always listen for the ''I'' in a person's statement.

*Conformity.* Poor teams stress conformity and a follow-the-rule approach, typically expressing this doctrine through statements such as the following: ''Don't rock the boat.'' ''The organization will take care of him.'' ''You haven't been here long enough. You'll learn.'' ''That's the way it is around here.''

*Tension Within Teams.* When people are uncomfortable together, and when the atmosphere is tense, a team is unable to
function in an open and sharing manner. Tension is manifested
in such nonverbal signs as wrinkled foreheads, tight fists, rigid
postures, curt voices, and so forth.

*Misunderstanding of Jobs or Roles.* Poorly functioning teams
produce members who express statements that convey confusion: "That's his job, not mine." "I have no idea why I'm
here." "Stay out of my territory. This is my job alone." When
people are working well together, they know and accept their
own roles and the roles of others; there are few job boundaries
that remain in dispute.

*Low Confidence in Others.* In an effective team, individuals not
only know the roles of other team members but also have confidence that other team members will carry out their parts of
the job. Comments such as the following express this confidence:
"You can count on Val." "You have our best person." "She
is reliable." "I'd stake my life on him."

*One-Person Decisions.* Poor teamwork can be a result of the way
team members participate in decisions. In poor teams, decisions
are boss-directed, with only marginal team-member input actually counting in final decisions. The people in the power positions, usually gained through political strategies, often manipulate a group to decide on the outcome they want; the use of
consensus is nearly nonexistent. As a result of this approach,
decisions are seldom accepted by the team, and when something
goes wrong, statements such as the following are heard: "That
wasn't my idea." "Don't you remember when you told us what
you wanted?" "Go talk to the guy who made the decision."

## The Importance of Recognizing Symptoms

An illustrative incident occurred in the maintenance department of a large, state-run university. The department was
made up of 175 custodians organized into teams of three to six
people each. Each team was responsible for a particular building

on campus. These teams had been intact for many years, with essentially the same crew chiefs and with relatively little personnel transfer from team to team. The department head responsible for custodial functions had received many complaints from the university's faculty and administration that their offices were not being properly cleaned: wastebaskets were not emptied, doors were left ajar, papers were rearranged within offices, and so forth. The complaints were coming from all parts of the campus, and they could not be tracked down to a particular team. During his rounds, the department head noted that members of the various teams tended to spend considerable time sitting and talking in their work rooms. When he observed the teams in action, they seemed to be working at a pace that he considered too sluggish. He was also aware of the fact that numerous members of various teams had expressed an interest in forming a union.

Given the circumstances, the department head decided to undertake a major reorganization of his custodial staff, restructuring the various teams and reassigning people from one team to another. He consulted briefly with his immediate superior about this change and received no objections, so he proceeded to initiate the reorganization. Within twenty-four hours, the vice-president of operations received a dozen phone calls protesting the reorganization, and a stinging petition was signed by more than one hundred members of the custodial staff, protesting the move and threatening to form a union. The petition was sent directly to the president and trustees of the university. The net result was that the department head in charge of custodial functions called off the change.

What the manager in this case failed to recognize was symptoms of a major problem in his organization. Instead of leaping forward and making changes as he did, he should have stepped back and asked himself, "What's going on here?" Had he taken the time to analyze the situation he was faced with, he would probably have taken very different action and avoided the nasty problem of explaining the petition. In the next chapter, we propose some ways that this type of problem can be analyzed and studied.

# 3

# Diagnosing Causes of
# Team Problems

A high-level manager at a large energy company sensed that problems were brewing among the members of his management team. Team members were not sharing information or ideas, and one particular member tended to be significantly more aggressive than the others, often taking over meetings and pushing forth his opinions. The reactions of team members to this aggressive personality exhibited what appeared to be a collective disgust. The manager concluded that the aggressive member was causing team problems and should be encouraged to take a less dominant position in the team. He therefore met with the member and told him that his "attitude needed to change" and that he should improve his interpersonal skills. The manager prescribed an outside training program that was designed to help managers become more aware of their impact on other people. Reluctantly, the member agreed to attend the training program.

Several weeks later, when the member returned from the training program, he adopted a very different posture within the team setting. In fact, the pendulum of his behavior had swung from very aggressive to highly submissive.

To the manager's surprise, however, most of the previously observed team problems continued. There were still strong indications that team members were holding back information and ideas, and the atmosphere of collective disgust remained. Faced with the persistence of team problems, the manager had to concede that his attempted solution had missed the mark and that one individual's aggressive behavior was not the root cause of the team's problems. In an effort to delve more deeply into the cause of the problems, he enlisted the aid of an outside consultant. Working together, they discovered that team members were experiencing a high level of frustration regarding their specific roles, the objectives of the team, and how particular objectives related to each individual role; they thus concluded that the failure to exchange information and ideas was due to the lack of clearly defined roles, functions, and objectives.

If attempts to correct problems are to be successful, managers must begin by collecting accurate and extensive data. Although it may be tempting to develop action plans based on readily accessible data, this is often the most counterproductive course a manager can take, since action based on incomplete information will rarely solve the root problem. The need for the systematic measurement and analysis of team problems *prior* to the development of action plans aimed at solving team problems cannot be overemphasized. The information measurement and analysis process involves three basic steps. The first step is recognizing the symptoms. The ability to recognize a potential problem within the team requires constant awareness on the part of a manager. Persistent symptoms send up flags, distress signals that indicate when a detailed analysis should be performed. The second step is to highlight and focus on the specific problem areas. Considering the numerous factors that influence the way teams function, the purpose of the highlighting process is to reveal the precise elements that are contributing to a given problem. The third step is to accurately define and clarify the exact problem in terms of its underlying cause-and-effect relationship, while taking into account the way in which people are reacting to the problem. If the problem has been fully and correctly dissected, an appropriate action plan can be drawn up to correct it; if the problem has not been properly defined, no solution will be possible. Once again, the medical model is applicable. If a physician incorrectly diagnoses a patient's illness, the prescribed remedy will likely be futile. The same principle applies to the diagnosis of team problems. If a manager misidentifies the origins and potential ramifications of a team problem, the proposed solution will most often be ineffective.

## Indicators of Team Productivity

There are several key elements that are commonly measured to develop a picture of how a team is functioning (Dyer, 1987; Rubin, Fry, and Plovich, 1978), and the following discussion provides a general guide. Obviously, additional elements can be examined, and sometimes only a select group of factors require study. Essentially, the nature of the problem determines the elements that need to be examined. However, as the range of elements to be investigated is reduced, the risk of overlooking pertinent factors is increased.

*Communication.* In an effective team, there are honest working relationships and high levels of trust. A healthy organization allows dissent and disagreement to be dealt with through a well-established and informal communication process. In such organizations, there are high listening levels, a sharing of information, appropriate praise exchanged between members, and feedback about how people are working together and meetings are being conducted. When people are working well together on an interpersonal level, effective decisions are reached with the least amount of effort, and the boss is open to suggestions and encourages the free expression of ideas and opinions.

*Objectives.* Effective teams have clear objectives that are understood by all team members. Members are committed to accomplishing these objectives, which are realistic yet challenging. In all cases, effective teams set goals through a process of participation and involvement.

*Interpersonal Conflict.* Interpersonal conflict is a natural part of the day-to-day interaction between people. In an effective team, there is a relatively low level of interpersonal conflict. When it does occur, it is not rigidly suppressed; rather, it is worked out in a healthy manner within the group.

*Organization.* An efficient team uses carefully designed formal and informal organizational approaches that are based on the functions of the team. These approaches are designed to fully utilize the abilities and skills of everyone on the team, while providing sufficient authority to get the job done and allowing enough flexibility for people to perform effectively.

*Controls.* Certain controls are built into the way an effective team functions. Performance standards are developed and agreed to in advance. These standards then become the measurements by which the actual performance of members is evaluated. Positive feedback is used to give team members information about their successes, and negative feedback is kept to a minimum.

*Support.* When a team is working well, a positive environment has been established by the members of the team, designed to respect and support the efforts of each member. This positive environment is candid and relaxed. Members of such a team feel at ease with each other and can honestly state their opinions.

*Roles of Team Members.* Effective teams make certain that members understand their respective roles and that these roles are agreed to and not imposed on members. Team members have confidence in themselves and express confidence in one another. There is a high degree of loyalty to the team, and this is often intensified when the team is under criticism from someone outside it.

*Decision Making.* When decisions are reached through consensus and all members feel that they have contributed to these decisions, an effective team is at work. The input from all members is carefully considered and evaluated, and final decisions are accepted by all members of the team.

*Results.* Increased productivity is the mark of a well-oiled team. When production information is always shared openly, team members are aware of and can control the factors that affect results.

## Gathering Information on Team Productivity

*Obstacles to Information Gathering.* Though managers confronted with the task of measuring and analyzing a difficult team problem frequently turn to the expertise of an outside consultant for assistance, managers themselves can accurately measure and analyze team problems if they carefully design their approach. Every manager who attempts to personally investigate a team problem must guard against certain pitfalls of subjectivity. One such pitfall is tunnel vision. Tunnel vision can prevent a manager from perceiving all the factors involved in a situation. Because of each individual's personal frame of reference, it is sometimes difficult to grasp the exact information that others are expressing. If a manager is unable to accurately visualize the problems that people describe from their frame of reference, then the manager will not fully comprehend the problems. For example, a manager might interpret a complaint that team members are being treated unfairly to mean that team members are not being paid fairly; certainly, this is not the only possible interpretation of such a statement. Tunnel vision can limit a manager's understanding of information, and a manager must be able to clearly discern the particulars of every situation. Preconceived bias can also cloud the perception of a manager. No manager can afford to retain outdated and unrealistic notions based on age, sex, creed, or color. If a manager is foolish enough to believe that a person's opinion is invalid simply because that type of person's opinion automatically lacks merit, that manager will never be able to correctly view a team problem. Every manager who is involved in a team situation will invariably have a less objective perception of the team's activities than will an outside observer. Someone who has no personal stake in the success or failure of a team will most often be capable of viewing information about the team with an impartial eye, more readily perceiving faults and areas that require improvement. Many managers tend to sidestep potentially volatile issues, preferring to avoid confrontation.

Questions of confidentiality can impede the flow of information. Because of the power position that a manager holds, people may tend to hold back information when reporting to the manager. If people feel that their honest opinions could somehow be used against them in the future, they will communicate in ciphers or clam up completely.

Despite these obstacles, it is still quite possible for a manager to handle data collection and analysis effectively, so long as the manager is aware of the various subjective obstacles and how they can inhibit the gathering of valid and reliable information. Much depends on team members' respect for and confidence in their manager. If there is a serious question as to how members of the team will react to the manager personally collecting the data, then use of a third party should be considered.

*Sources of Information.* Among the most effective of the variety of techniques used to gather information are direct observation, interviews, and questionnaires. Direct observation has the advantage of being casual, informal, and less disruptive to the organization than other approaches. The disadvantages of this method are that it is fairly unreliable and that it can miss much of the data available through more controlled measurement approaches. Because feelings and attitudes lie behind the observable behaviors of people, it is quite possible to draw the wrong inference from these behaviors. The interview process is more suited to uncovering underlying feelings and attitudes. Interviews provide substantial data along with an in-depth picture of what is going on within the team. However, interviews take time, and if the manager personally conducts the interviews, data may be withheld for fear of reprisal. Other sources of information include productivity records, minutes of meetings, customer complaints, and so forth. These sources tend to be indirect indicators of teamwork; thus, any problems they seem to uncover must be explored further before conclusions are drawn.

Questionnaires are most commonly relied on as sources of information about the team. They have the advantage of keeping the measurement process relatively objective. They also render data in a quantifiable form, and people tend to feel relatively comfortable in stating their opinions through questionnaires. Questionnaires are frequently used to highlight the areas that center around a team problem. There are numerous standardized questionnaires that can be used to collect data about teams. (Exhibits 1 and 2 provide typical examples.) When using standardized questionnaires, a manager must remain aware of their inherent limitations: the questionnaire may not be measuring all the factors that need to be examined; it may not contain terminology common to the particular organization that is being surveyed; and it may generate negative reactions on the part of team members if they feel that it is not tailored to the specific needs of their organization.

Though standardized questionnaires, when properly introduced and explained, can serve as effective tools to highlight problems within the organizational context, managers frequently feel that designing their own questionnaire is the best approach to a problem. The design process typically begins with assembling a list of specifics that should be examined in the questionnaire. The list is usually assembled through one or both of two methods: a passive observation of the systems functioning within the team and/or an unobtrusive probing of members of the team to determine which factors require examination. There are also numerous methods through which team members can directly provide a list of factors that should be studied. Two productive approaches of this type are brainstorming and storyboarding. Through brainstorming, which means throwing out ideas with no mutual attempt to screen them, team members often expose elements that may have previously escaped examination. The storyboarding process is a bit more organized. With this method, members of the team come up with questions that they feel should be contained in the questionnaire and write down each question on a card. The cards are then fastened to a board, and team members examine, clarify, and prioritize them. Once the questions have been organized, an accurate and useful questionnaire can be constructed. When team members are involved in the general design of a questionnaire, they are more accepting of the concepts involved in teamwork measurement and have a better understanding of what the questionnaire is attempting to measure, so that their answers are more straightforward and accurate.

Every questionnaire design should be consistent and focused. Peripheral questions should not be included, as the purpose of a questionnaire is to provide reliable data for future analysis; a detailed and complete analysis cannot be conducted if gratuitous elements are included in the questionnaire.

*Collecting the Information.* There are three basic steps involved in collecting information that will accurately highlight the problem area: preparation, collection, and summarization. These steps can be performed by the manager alone or with the aid of a third party.

1. *Preparation.* Even if the problem is not yet fully understood, an agreement must first be reached that a problem does exist. Once the problem has been acknowledged, the team should be involved in the process of determining how the problem can best be measured. This process should include a comparison of various measurement approaches. Team involvement will promote a commitment to solving the problem and an understanding of how to go about it. Members will develop a greater awareness of team problems and will become more inclined to share their views. If a team is not committed to the effort, there is a high risk that invalid information will be received and that considerable resistance will be encountered.

2. *Collection.* A manager who elects to personally conduct the survey needs to consider how the questionnaire should be distributed, how it should be returned, how to guard against breach of anonymity, and who will process the information. It is important to have more than one member of the team involved in the collection process. If only one person controls the collection process, especially if it is the manager, other members might feel that the data could somehow be misinterpreted, misunderstood, or misused.

3. *Summarization.* The collected information should be organized into a format that presents the results concisely and vividly; this will enable team members to immediately recognize the areas that need improvement. The specific purpose of the summarization process is to illuminate elements that require further work. Visual graphics (bar charts, percentage distributions,

and so forth) are very useful tools for presenting the data in a readily digestible form.

*Analyzing the Information.* Once the team is able to focus on the problem, analysis should begin. A manager should not attempt to dominate the analyzing process. A manager who attempts to dictate the meaning of data results to team members without asking for their input risks being accused of bias and of not giving individual members an opportunity to share their views. Getting people involved produces ownership of the problem and eventually of the proposed solution. The most acceptable and appropriate approach is to present the data to the team members and ask them to comment on areas that they feel should be dealt with more completely. As analysis proceeds and problems come into sharper focus, possible solutions begin to emerge.

Analysis of data typically follows the problem-solving format illustrated in Exhibits 3 through 5. In this example, a management team completed a teamwork survey (Exhibit 3) and consolidated the data into a report. The team then met as a group and identified the problem areas using the analysis form shown in Exhibit 4. This form provided a means to sort out the questions in each area (task, process, interpersonal, and leadership) that had the most negative and neutral responses. Finally, the group organized the data into problem categories and arranged the categories according to the priority of attention they should receive (Exhibit 5). The result of this effort was the identification of areas that need the team's immediate attention.

The next step is to understand what this information means (definition of the problem) and to devise ways to solve the problem (action planning). This is discussed in Chapter Four.

## Exhibit 1. Team Profile Questionnaire.

Indicate your extent of agreement with each of the statements below by assigning a number (1 through 5) to each in the right margin.
1 = strongly disagree, 2 = disagree, 3 = don't know, 4 = agree, 5 = strongly agree.

*Extent of Agreement*

1. The present goals and objectives of this team are clear and relevant to its overall mission. _____

2. Role definitions are clear so that there are seldom any misunderstandings about who is responsible for what. _____

3. Decisions are made on a timely basis with adequate opportunity for input and consideration by those affected. _____

4. There is a relatively high level of disclosure among team members, with a belief that the facts are usually "friendly" and in the long run it is better to deal with reality than to deny, avoid, or distort it. _____

5. Team members have a high awareness of the impact of their behavior on their environment and have open lines of communication with each other. _____

6. Team members are skilled at diagnosing and working on team problems; members attend to the process as well as the content of their meetings. _____

7. Mistakes are not punished but rather are viewed as opportunities to learn; risk is accepted as a condition of growth and change. _____

8. Team leadership is flexible, shifting in style to suit the needs of the situation and the people involved. _____

9. Collaboration is entered into freely, and ways of helping one another are highly developed. _____

10. The team is able to focus energies on appropriate priorities, not just respond to the most urgent crisis or follow the plan simply because it is there. _____

11. Relationships are honest; interpersonal issues are confronted rather than swept under the rug. _____

12. There are high awareness and effective use of available resources by team members. _____

13. There is good awareness of the interdependencies among team members, and collaboration rather than competition predominates. _____

14. Team norms foster creativity; members are not locked into past traditions and are able to bring fresh perspectives to present problems. _____

15. Conflicts are considered a normal part of working together and are dealt with openly and honestly. _____

16. Problem solving is pragmatic and informal; the boss is frequently challenged, and status and territorial rights take a backseat to the requirements of the problem. _____

17. Planning is considered an essential activity, and all team members participate actively in the process. _____

Exhibit 1. Team Profile Questionnaire, Cont'd.

18.   The team provides a supportive environment for its members
      to realize their uniqueness by allowing for and encouraging in-
      dividual differences.                                        _____

19.   The overall trust level is high, as evidenced by a healthy amount
      of confronting, spontaneity, and risk taking in meetings.     _____

## Exhibit 2. Analyzing Team Effectiveness.

This form is designed to stimulate an analysis and discussion of how well your team is functioning. There are two factors represented in this form that determine a team's effectiveness. Section I analyzes the team's *task*—what the team accomplished, whether goals were achieved and deadlines met, and so on. Section II analyzes the team's *process*—how the team performs its tasks, how decisions are made, how communications are handled, the planning process, and so on. For each subject, please indicate your rating and briefly state your reasons for it.

### Section I: Task

*Rating Scale:*

| 1 | 2 | 3 | 4 | 5 |
|---|---|---|---|---|
| Team does not meet task requirements. | Team meets some task requirements. | Team meets the major task requirements. | Team meets all task requirements. | Team consistently exceeds expectations. |

1. *Planning and organizing*
   How well does the planning and organizing of this team
   prepare it to accomplish its tasks?                          1 2 3 4 5
   Comments:

2. *Problem definition and solution*
   How well does this team define and solve the problems it
   faces?                                                       1 2 3 4 5
   Comments:

3. *Control*
   How effective are the controls that this team establishes to
   ensure that results are achieved as planned?                 1 2 3 4 5
   Comments:

4. *Goals and objectives*
   How well does this team meet the goals and objectives it
   establishes?                                                 1 2 3 4 5
   Comments:

5. *Follow-up*
   How well does this team follow up or take corrective action
   when needed?                                                 1 2 3 4 5
   Comments:

Exhibit 2. Analyzing Team Effectiveness, Cont'd.

## Section II: Process

*Rating Scale:* 1 = minimal teamwork conditions, 5 = ideal teamwork conditions

1.  *Listening*
    Members don't really listen
    to each other, interrupt.                    1 2 3 4 5       All members really listen, try
                                                                 hard to understand, and are
                                                                 understood.

    Comments:

2.  *Communications*
    Communications are
    guarded, cautious.                           1 2 3 4 5       Communications are open,
    Comments:                                                    authentic.

3.  *Attitudes toward differences*
    *within group*
    Members avoid arguments,                                     Members search for respect
    smooth over differences,     1 2 3 4 5                       and accept differences and
    avoid conflicts.                                             work them through openly as
                                                                 a team.

    Comments:

4.  *Involvement and participation*
    Discussion is dominated by                   1 2 3 4 5       All members are involved,
    a few members.                                               free to participate in the way
                                                                 they want.

    Comments:

5.  *Commitment*
    There is little commitment to                1 2 3 4 5       All members are highly com-
    team effort.                                                 mitted to the team's effort.
                                                                 All work hard to get a good
                                                                 team solution and are com-
                                                                 mitted to the team's de-
                                                                 cisions.

    Comments:

6.  *Mutual support*
    There is indifference to                     1 2 3 4 5       Members get help from
    needs or concerns of others.                                 others on the team and give
                                                                 help; they have genuine con-
                                                                 cern for each other.

    Comments:

7.  *Flexibility*
    Group is locked in on                                        Members readily change
    established rules. Members                                   procedures to meet situation.
    find it hard to change pro-   1 2 3 4 5
    cedures.
    Comments:

## Exhibit 3. Teamwork Survey.

Team leader's name: _____

Your name: _____

Your age: _____    Date survey completed: _____

Your education level: ___ High School ___ B.S./B.A. ___ Master's ___ Ph.D.

Your length of service (years): _____

Location: _____

### INSTRUCTIONS:

You and other members of your team have been asked to fill out this Teamwork Survey to assist your team in improving its productivity. It is important that you carefully fill the survey out within the next one or two days and return it in the attached envelope. Responses will be summarized into a team profile so that your individual responses cannot be identified.

Note that for each item in the survey, the statement on the left is the opposite of the statement on the right. Between the two statements are five blank circles. The middle circle is intended to reflect neutral feelings toward the statement. The circles to the left of the middle circle indicate degrees of agreement with the statement on the left. The two circles to the right of the middle circle indicate degrees of agreement with the statement on the right. Please indicate your views by filling in only one circle per item.

For example, item 1 reads:

1.  Communications on my      ○ ○ ○ ○ ○      Communications on my
    team are generally                        team are generally open.
    guarded.

The circles represent ranges of agreement:

| ○ | ○ | ○ | ○ | ○ |
|---|---|---|---|---|
| I strongly agree with the statement on the left. | I agree with the statement on the left. | I am neutral. | I agree with the statement on the right. | I strongly agree with the statement on the right. |

So for item 1, if you feel that your team's communication is pretty open, you would mark the fourth circle, indicating "I agree with the statement on the right." If you believe, however, that communication on your team is very guarded, you would mark the first circle, indicating strong agreement with the statement on the left.

As you fill in your responses, think of your team as a whole and the way the team works together. If you are a team leader, think of yourself as a part of the team when you respond to the questions.

Your thoughtful participation is greatly appreciated.

Exhibit 3. Teamwork Survey, Cont'd.

1.  Communications on my          ○ ○ ○ ○ ○   Communications on my
    team are generally                        team are generally open.
    guarded.

2.  I do not know what my         ○ ○ ○ ○ ○   I know what my team's
    team's objectives are.                    objectives are.

3.  I am rewarded for             ○ ○ ○ ○ ○   I am not rewarded for in-
    innovating or improving                   novating or improving
    things that benefit my                    things that benefit my
    team.                                     team.

4.  Members of my team do         ○ ○ ○ ○ ○   Members of my team
    not have confidence in                    have confidence in each
    each other.                               other.

5.  My team's objectives are      ○ ○ ○ ○ ○   My team's objectives are
    not attainable.                           attainable.

6.  My team has no set            ○ ○ ○ ○ ○   My team has set pro-
    procedures for solving                    cedures for solving
    problems.                                 problems.

7.  My team does not have a       ○ ○ ○ ○ ○   My team has a well-
    well-defined system for                   defined system for com-
    communicating to other                    municating to other team
    team members.                             members.

8.  My team leader and I do       ○ ○ ○ ○ ○   My team leader and I
    not agree on my job                       agree on my job
    objectives.                               objectives.

9.  My team spends much of        ○ ○ ○ ○ ○   My team takes the time
    its time "fire fighting."                 to plan ahead and thereby
                                              avoids "fire fighting."

10. My team leader tends to       ○ ○ ○ ○ ○   My team leader en-
    dominate decision                         courages team participa-
    making.                                   tion in decision making.

11. My abilities, knowledge,      ○ ○ ○ ○ ○   My abilities, knowledge,
    and experience are not                    and experience are fully
    utilized by my team.                      utilized by my team.

12. Members of my team do         ○ ○ ○ ○ ○   Members of my team
    not trust each other.                     trust each other.

13. I do not understand my        ○ ○ ○ ○ ○   I clearly understand my
    role on this team.                        role on this team.

14. My team pressures             ○ ○ ○ ○ ○   My team encourages in-
    members to conform to                     dividual differences.
    group norms.

## Exhibit 3. Teamwork Survey, Cont'd.

15. I do not understand my job objectives relative to my team's objectives.    ○ ○ ○ ○ ○    I understand my job objectives relative to my team's objectives.

16. The work climate on my team is relaxed.    ○ ○ ○ ○ ○    The work climate on my team is tense.

17. Team meetings are poorly organized.    ○ ○ ○ ○ ○    Team meetings are well organized.

18. I am committed to my job objectives.    ○ ○ ○ ○ ○    I am not committed to my job objectives.

19. Members of my team are loyal to the team.    ○ ○ ○ ○ ○    Members of my team are not loyal to the team.

20. Team members generally do not listen to each other.    ○ ○ ○ ○ ○    Team members generally listen to each other.

21. When an interpersonal issue is raised on the team, we avoid it.    ○ ○ ○ ○ ○    When an interpersonal issue is raised on the team, we have procedures for resolving it.

22. I receive feedback frequently.    ○ ○ ○ ○ ○    I receive feedback infrequently.

23. My job objectives are challenging.    ○ ○ ○ ○ ○    My job objectives are not challenging.

24. I agree with my role on my team.    ○ ○ ○ ○ ○    I do not agree with my role on my team.

25. There is little evidence of conflict between team members.    ○ ○ ○ ○ ○    There is much evidence of conflict between team members.

26. My team leader is open to suggestions on how to improve his or her performance.    ○ ○ ○ ○ ○    My team leader is not open to suggestions on how to improve his or her performance.

27. I am satisfied with my team's productivity.    ○ ○ ○ ○ ○    I am not satisfied with my team's productivity.

28. I am not given enough authority to do my job.    ○ ○ ○ ○ ○    I am given sufficient authority to do my job.

29. I do not feel that my team leader considers my input when making decisions.    ○ ○ ○ ○ ○    I feel that my team leader considers my input when making decisions.

Exhibit 3. Teamwork Survey, Cont'd.

| | | | |
|---|---|---|---|
| 30. | I do not understand the roles of my fellow team members. | ○ ○ ○ ○ ○ | I understand the roles of my fellow team members. |
| 31. | My team's productivity is generally low. | ○ ○ ○ ○ ○ | My team's productivity is generally high. |
| 32. | I hesitate to be candid with my fellow team members. | ○ ○ ○ ○ ○ | I feel free to be candid with my fellow team members. |
| 33. | My performance evaluations are based on my performance. | ○ ○ ○ ○ ○ | My performance evaluations are not based on my performance. |
| 34. | Consensus is rarely reached within my team. | ○ ○ ○ ○ ○ | Consensus is usually reached within my team. |
| 35. | Team members are generally uncooperative. | ○ ○ ○ ○ ○ | Team members are generally cooperative. |
| 36. | Team members are unclear about how we are expected to make decisions. | ○ ○ ○ ○ ○ | Team members are clear about how we are expected to make decisions. |
| 37. | My job objectives are not attainable. | ○ ○ ○ ○ ○ | My job objectives are attainable. |
| 38. | Decisions often are not explained to members of my team. | ○ ○ ○ ○ ○ | Decisions usually are explained to members of my team. |
| 39. | Praise is seldom provided for a job well done. | ○ ○ ○ ○ ○ | Praise is usually provided for a job well done. |
| 40. | My team encourages me to improve my skills. | ○ ○ ○ ○ ○ | My team does not encourage me to improve my skills. |
| 41. | Feedback on my team is usually negative and destructive. | ○ ○ ○ ○ ○ | Feedback on my team is usually positive and helpful. |
| 42. | Team meetings are generally unproductive, with few conclusions drawn or decisions made. | ○ ○ ○ ○ ○ | Team meetings are generally productive, with conclusions drawn and decisions made. |
| 43. | My team does not have a sense of direction. | ○ ○ ○ ○ ○ | My team has developed a clear sense of direction. |

Exhibit 4. Analysis of Teamwork Survey.

## Roles

*Question 13*   I do / do not understand my role on team.

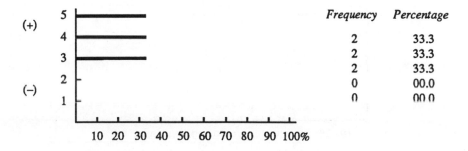

| | Frequency | Percentage |
|---|---|---|
| | 2 | 33.3 |
| | 2 | 33.3 |
| | 2 | 33.3 |
| | 0 | 00.0 |
| | 0 | 00.0 |

*Question 24*   I do / do not agree with my role on team.

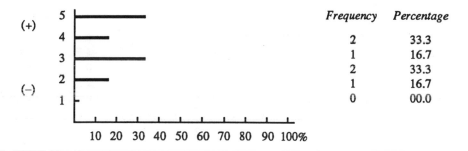

| | Frequency | Percentage |
|---|---|---|
| | 2 | 33.3 |
| | 1 | 16.7 |
| | 2 | 33.3 |
| | 1 | 16.7 |
| | 0 | 00.0 |

*Question 30*   I do / do not understand roles of team members.

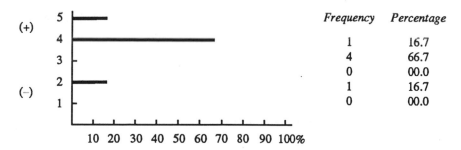

| | Frequency | Percentage |
|---|---|---|
| | 1 | 16.7 |
| | 4 | 66.7 |
| | 0 | 00.0 |
| | 1 | 16.7 |
| | 0 | 00.0 |

Exhibit 4. Analysis of Teamwork Survey, Cont'd.

## Objectives

*Question 2*     I do / do not know team's objectives.

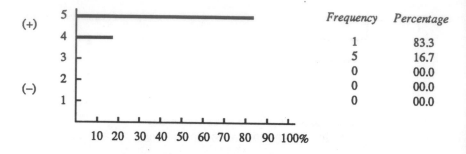

| | Frequency | Percentage |
|---|---|---|
| | 1 | 83.3 |
| | 5 | 16.7 |
| | 0 | 00.0 |
| | 0 | 00.0 |
| | 0 | 00.0 |

*Question 5*     My team's objectives are / are not attainable.

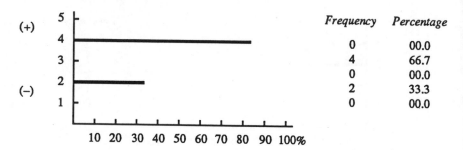

| | Frequency | Percentage |
|---|---|---|
| | 0 | 00.0 |
| | 4 | 66.7 |
| | 0 | 00.0 |
| | 2 | 33.3 |
| | 0 | 00.0 |

*Question 8*     My team leader and I do / do not agree on job objectives.

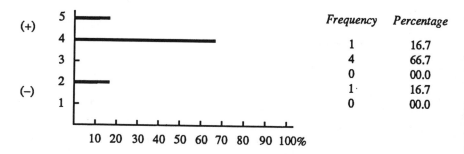

| | Frequency | Percentage |
|---|---|---|
| | 1 | 16.7 |
| | 4 | 66.7 |
| | 0 | 00.0 |
| | 1 | 16.7 |
| | 0 | 00.0 |

Exhibit 4. Analysis of Teamwork Survey, Cont'd.

*Question 15*    I do / do not understand my job objectives relative to team's objectives.

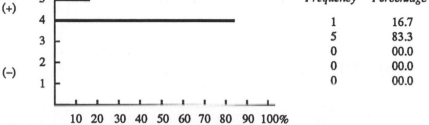

| | Frequency | Percentage |
|---|---|---|
| | 1 | 16.7 |
| | 5 | 83.3 |
| | 0 | 00.0 |
| | 0 | 00.0 |
| | 0 | 00.0 |

*Question 18*    I am / am not committed to my job objectives.

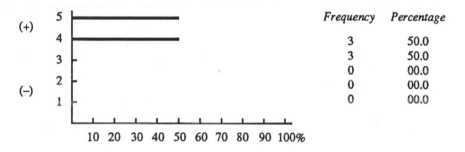

| | Frequency | Percentage |
|---|---|---|
| | 3 | 50.0 |
| | 3 | 50.0 |
| | 0 | 00.0 |
| | 0 | 00.0 |
| | 0 | 00.0 |

*Question 23*    My job objectives are / are not challenging.

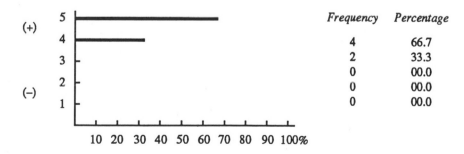

| | Frequency | Percentage |
|---|---|---|
| | 4 | 66.7 |
| | 2 | 33.3 |
| | 0 | 00.0 |
| | 0 | 00.0 |
| | 0 | 00.0 |

Exhibit 4. Analysis of Teamwork Survey, Cont'd.

*Question 37*　My job objectives are / are not attainable.

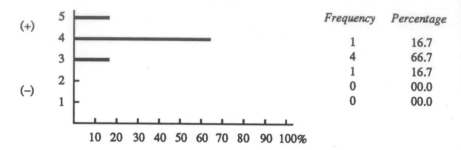

| | Frequency | Percentage |
|---|---|---|
| | 1 | 16.7 |
| | 4 | 66.7 |
| | 1 | 16.7 |
| | 0 | 00.0 |
| | 0 | 00.0 |

## Abilities/Skills/Knowledge

*Question 11*　My abilities, knowledge, and experience are / are not utilized by team.

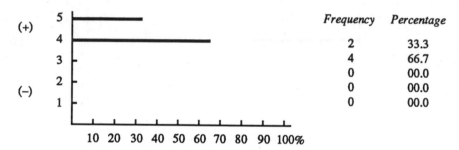

| | Frequency | Percentage |
|---|---|---|
| | 2 | 33.3 |
| | 4 | 66.7 |
| | 0 | 00.0 |
| | 0 | 00.0 |
| | 0 | 00.0 |

## Authority to Do Job

*Question 28*　I am / am not given authority to do the job.

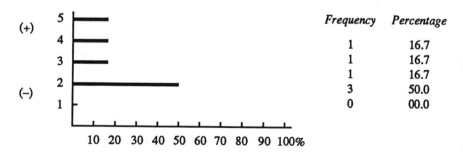

| | Frequency | Percentage |
|---|---|---|
| | 1 | 16.7 |
| | 1 | 16.7 |
| | 1 | 16.7 |
| | 3 | 50.0 |
| | 0 | 00.0 |

## Exhibit 5. Teamwork Survey Action Plan.

### Task

| | Question | Your Decision | | | Team Decision |
|---|---|---|---|---|---|
| | | Take Action Now | Take Action Later | No Action Required | |
| Roles | 13 | _____ | ×___ | _____ | |
| | 24 | ×___ | _____ | _____ | |
| | 30 | _____ | ×___ | _____ | |
| Objectives | 2 | _____ | _____ | ×___ | |
| | 5 | ×___ | _____ | _____ | |
| | 8 | _____ | ×___ | _____ | |
| | 15 | _____ | _____ | ×___ | |
| | 18 | _____ | _____ | ×___ | |
| | 23 | _____ | _____ | ×___ | |
| | 37 | _____ | _____ | ×___ | |
| Abilities | 11 | _____ | _____ | ×___ | |
| Authority | 28 | ×___ | _____ | _____ | |

### Process

| Question | Your Decision | | | Team Decision |
|---|---|---|---|---|
| | Take Action Now | Take Action Later | No Action Required | |
| 6 | _____ | _____ | _____ | |
| 7 | _____ | _____ | _____ | |
| 9 | _____ | _____ | _____ | |
| 17 | _____ | _____ | _____ | |
| 21 | _____ | _____ | _____ | |
| 36 | _____ | _____ | _____ | |
| 43 | _____ | _____ | _____ | |

## Exhibit 5. Teamwork Survey Action Plan, Cont'd.

### Interpersonal

| | Your Decision | | | |
|---|---|---|---|---|
| Question | Take Action Now | Take Action Later | No Action Required | Team Decision |
| 1 | ___ | ___ | ___ | |
| 4 | ___ | ___ | ___ | |
| 12 | ___ | ___ | ___ | |
| 14 | ___ | ___ | ___ | |
| 16 | ___ | ___ | ___ | |
| 19 | ___ | ___ | ___ | |
| 20 | ___ | ___ | ___ | |
| 25 | ___ | ___ | ___ | |
| 32 | ___ | ___ | ___ | |
| 35 | ___ | ___ | ___ | |
| 40 | ___ | ___ | ___ | |

### Leadership

| | Your Decision | | | |
|---|---|---|---|---|
| Question | Take Action Now | Take Action Later | No Action Required | Team Decision |
| 10 | ___ | ___ | ___ | |
| 22 | ___ | ___ | ___ | |
| 26 | ___ | ___ | ___ | |
| 29 | ___ | ___ | ___ | |
| 33 | ___ | ___ | ___ | |
| 34 | ___ | ___ | ___ | |
| 38 | ___ | ___ | ___ | |
| 39 | ___ | ___ | ___ | |
| 41 | ___ | ___ | ___ | |

# ❧ 4 ❧

# Action Planning
# for Team Improvement

Of all the phases involved in improving team effectiveness, the process of transforming information into action is certainly one of the most important. Once collected data has brought the specific problem to light, it is time to put this knowledge to work. This process involves four steps: fleshing out a complete definition of the problem, determining which plan of action is best suited to correcting the problem, implementing the most appropriate plan, and evaluating the overall effectiveness of the action. It is essential to the success of this process that an accurate and thorough definition be developed and that the plan of action be designed to eliminate the root cause of the specific problem. If the crucial link between information and action is missing, then improvement in team effectiveness will not be achieved.

## Definition of the Problem

The clear and accurate definition of any problem is fundamental to improving teamwork. If a precise understanding of the cause-and-effect relationships rooted within the structure of a team is not reached, then it is highly improbable that team problems will be corrected. Because most managers have been taught to be decisive and to act quickly on information, many are tempted to hastily interpret the data obtained from a preliminary survey and immediately chart a plan of action based on this inadequate interpretation. Whenever a manager elects to implement an action plan derived from an incomplete assessment, it is quite likely that the problem will only be compounded.

43

A comprehensive definition of team problems requires the contributions of team members. Managers usually do not possess or do not understand all the relevant information; additional information must be solicited from the team. Team members are the ones most able to amplify and clarify the collected information, especially the information that they themselves provided. Managers can mishandle data that appear crystal clear if they do not double-check with team members to guarantee validity and to ensure that the data accurately reflect the team members' concerns. When team members can confirm the definition through their own experiences, the problem has been clearly identified. Once managers have garnered the information that team members have to offer and the problem has been openly discussed and thoughtfully examined, corrective plans of action become easier to identify and define.

The involvement of team members in the process of defining a problem in itself tends to improve team effectiveness. If managers have not previously included their teams in this type of activity, team members usually have a strong desire to participate in determining the team's direction. Getting the team involved in the definition of the problem utilizes the forces of group dynamics and positive interaction. Team involvement also usually results in stronger support for the suggested change and a greater commitment to solving the problem.

One of the most productive approaches for getting a team involved is to present the raw data to the team, succinctly explaining how the data were summarized and formulated, and then to open up a discussion on the areas of primary concern (that is, those that received the lowest questionnaire ratings from team members). Although it is tempting to address a number of areas, lines must be drawn that limit examination to the issues of prime importance. Team members should be encouraged to focus on top-priority components of the problem; their efforts should not be overextended. Managers and teams have a tendency to immediately take on all problems, instead of dealing with them one at a time in the order of their importance.

Once the primary components of a problem have been identified, the team should concentrate on the specifics of each component, tackling the most important areas first and probing for further clarification of the factors that are contributing to the problem. This process is greatly enhanced when team members are asked to relate actual examples of behavior. Team members should be discouraged from being overcritical of each other's comments. An overall openness must be maintained in order to prevent hesitation, reservation, or other defensive behaviors.

An example of this process is a team that has identified the quality of team meetings as one of its primary problems. To translate this into more specific terms, the team considers the question "What exactly are the reasons that members of the team believe meetings are poorly conducted?" All team members are given the opportunity to contribute their understanding of what causes the problem, and the following explanations might be suggested: "We don't have an agenda," "We don't reach decisions at the end of our meetings," and "Meetings are unnecessarily long." Once the problem has been described in these more specific terms, further details are sought, and team members are encouraged to provide examples.

The more precise the definition, the more likely that the problem will be corrected. Trying to move ahead with a cloudy definition of a problem is like trying to maneuver along a winding road in the rain without windshield wipers. There are several steps that can facilitate the development of a clear definition of team problems. First, always get specifics, and strive for examples that illustrate those specifics. Second, attempt to reach consensus. It is important that all members of a team recognize and agree on the nature of a problem. Finally, avoid placing heavy blame on team members who may be contributing to the problem. At this point, information, not rectification, is what must be sought.

## Action Planning

Always decide what actions need to be taken on the basis of facts rather than inference. It is easy to draw inferences from limited data, but wild guesses should never be acted on. Depend only on objective, specific, and comprehensive information as a guide for establishing corrective measures.

In one company, a team that had previously been highly productive suddenly began to display a sharp decrease in results. The supervisor of the group assumed that team members were starting to goof off and began issuing stern directives calling for more attentive work practices. Productivity did not improve, however, and so a representative from the human resources department was asked to look into the matter. The investigation pointed directly at a change in lighting that had been instituted to reduce energy costs, which made it more difficult for the workers to see. The poor lighting forced team members to become cautious in their work, and this was the cause of the slump in productivity.

Once a problem has been clearly defined, the process of developing a solution begins. Numerous methods can be used to explore the possible approaches to planned action. Obviously, the manager must have a working knowledge of the proven action plans that are available. It is also indispensable that team members be involved in the selection of the action plan. It is important that a consensus be developed among team members on how the problem should be solved. A discussion process should be used to elicit team members' reactions to proposed solutions and the reasons behind their opinions. The process should continue until all members agree on a particular approach. Then individual members should be assigned specific responsibilities for implementing the action plans that have been selected, and time frames should be set so that the team can measure progress toward correction. In addition, a method of evaluation must be established that will indicate whether the problem has been solved.

To illustrate the process of the transformation of information into action, we will return to the example provided earlier of the team dealing with the problem of unproductive team meetings. The team members had broken the problem down into three primary components: lack of agenda, failure to reach decisions, and domination of meetings by particular members. Through a brainstorming session, the team determined that an agenda should be established twenty-four hours in advance of each meeting. All members could contribute items to the agenda, as long as they submitted them by the twenty-four-hour deadline. The agenda would rank items in order of importance and indicate the amount of time to be spent on each issue. It would be typed up and distributed as soon as possible so that all the team members would be familiar with it when they met.

The second component of the team's problem, failure to reach decisions, was addressed through a problem-solving approach. The manager identified which decisions will be made solely by the manager and which will be the shared responsibility of the team. Clarifications such as this will enable the group to be more decisive, as very little time will be wasted on constantly reestablishing responsibilities.

To curtail the domination of meetings by aggressive individuals, the team decided to end each meeting with a brief discussion of the processes followed during the meeting, including an examination of team members' participation in the meeting. During such discussions, it was determined that team members should avoid pointing the finger at particular individuals; the manager should rely on the general power of the group to influence members to alter counterproductive behaviors. This was a wise decision, because as a team develops into a cohesive unit, mutual feedback among members becomes an invaluable tool. Fledgling teams, however, should wait until a positive commitment has been established.

To implement these three plans, the team chose two members to work on the agenda, the manager agreed to work on the decision-making process, and the group reached a general agreement that committed all members to more participative and interactive meetings. The team established a time schedule for adopting the new agenda process and for the manager's assessment of his role in the decision-making process. They agreed to hold a follow-up meeting a month and a half later to discuss the progress of the plans and to conduct a follow-up survey at the end of six months to determine whether there were significant signs of improvement.

## Implementation, Follow-Up, and Review of Progress

If a clear definition of the problem has been developed and appropriate action steps have been formulated, the implementation process becomes relatively straightforward. However, it is important to ensure that some sort of monitoring process is established. Such a process usually involves team members taking responsibility for overseeing how well the plan is being implemented and continuing to raise questions about whether the team is accomplishing its goals. Evaluation can be conducted both through individual monitoring and on a group level through continued discussion and surveying. Continued surveying has the advantages of providing quantitative and tangible results and guarding against stagnation on the part of team members. Joint efforts to solve problems and positive signs of improvement have a stimulating effect on a team and make the team more cohesive and productive.

Never place teamwork problems on the back burner. Although it may be tempting to view the interactions, structure, and chemistry of a team as secondary to the task that the team is trying to accomplish, team dynamics are intimately linked to the ability of a team to achieve its goals. You cannot travel far in a poorly tuned car. To prevent slipping into the trap of setting aside team problems, the importance of building an effective team should be established at the outset.

# ✿ 5 ✿

# Defining Team Member
# Roles and Responsibilities

Defining roles and responsibilities is one of the most challenging problems that today's teams must tackle. There are three specific reasons why this is so important and demanding: (1) When a team's problems are carefully studied and examined, the sources of the problems more often than not are found to involve the lack of clearly defined roles. (2) The ability of a team to correct problems involving roles and responsibilities is a collective skill that can readily be improved, and most teams are willing to address it. (3) Because there are a large number of texts, seminars, and workshops concerned with defining roles and responsibilities, information on this subject is readily available for managers to study.

The importance of clearly defined roles and responsibilities is felt daily in every business situation. In one very large company, the primary goal of the engineering department was to produce designs that would improve the flow of fluids through certain pieces of equipment. The engineers were expected to accomplish this task within six months. The manager of the department had explained this goal to each engineer individually, first outlining the broad goal and then specifically identifying the responsibilities and targets of the particular individual. However, he did not discuss the task with the group as a whole. Considerable confusion soon arose. One engineer understood that he was supposed to speed up the flow of fluids by $X$ amount by the end of three weeks; another engineer assumed that his task was to slow down the flow of fluids by $X$ amount by the

49

end of three weeks. Working independently and in isolation from the other, the two engineers invested much time and energy in the completion of their designs. When the two designs were brought together, the manager was flabbergasted to discover that they were in total contradiction and absurdly incompatible. He called the two engineers together and asked how they had come up with designs that were direct opposites; each engineer responded, "I only did what I was told to do." Obviously, if two members of the same team are diligently working in completely opposite directions, firmly believing that their endeavors are best for the team, the manager has not clearly defined roles, responsibilities, and goals.

There are two basic types of roles and responsibilities that need to be evaluated: those involving the job or task and those involving management of the processes of the team. Establishing clear task definition begins with understanding the role expectations of each individual. When a group of people are interacting and confronting a common problem, they usually express considerable interest in the dynamics and complexities of individuals' perceptions of their roles and how they correlate with each other. Role perception relates directly to the personality characteristics and personal histories of the individuals involved.

Managers must be aware of the fact that individuals have expectations and anticipations concerning their own roles, as well as the roles of others on the team. Early on in the establishment of a team, it is advisable to ask members to express their expectations and anticipations. When this information is brought to light at the outset, numerous potential problems can be avoided, and members of the team will be able to more easily accept and fulfill their respective roles.

During any discussion of roles and responsibilities, all members of a team should come to clearly understand their specific tasks and the areas for which they will be held accountable. Such a discussion should lead members of the team into positions that will result in strength and mutual support. When each member understands what the others are going to be held accountable for, team members will be unlikely to perceive their roles as independent of other members of the team.

## Role Clarification

Role clarification should be conducted when a new team is formed, when a new task is to be accomplished by the team, or whenever significant changes in circumstances require reassignment of responsibilities. Although job descriptions are frequently consulted, they should not serve as the sole criteria of performance. Role clarification should be carried out with the purpose of understanding and establishing the responsibilities and roles of individuals on a team, and this is best accomplished through a verbal give and take. Generally, a manager should not simply send out memos in an attempt to clarify roles.

It is only natural that a certain amount of conflict and disruption will arise as people attempt to clarify the definitions of their own roles. Such differences must be dealt with on a situational basis, as each point of contention will require a separate method of correction. The roles and responsibilities of each member must be considered and examined within the context of the whole team so that it is possible to determine whether the necessary functions have been assigned in a way that enables the team to successfully carry out all its tasks and projects. To achieve this, it is necessary to analyze the overall design and intention of the team and then to break down the general task into its individual components.

While roles are not clearly defined, numerous problems can arise: work not yet accomplished becomes a major stumbling block; task assignments are often redundant and overlapping; gaps exist where tasks have not been assigned; a significant amount of buck passing and backbiting can arise; there is little mutual support; activities are poorly coordinated; and it is extremely difficult for managers to pinpoint which individuals are not meeting their responsibilities. A relatively straightforward and simple process that a manager can utilize to develop role clarification, known as role negotiation, is outlined below (Hill, 1982).

*Definition.* Role negotiation is a process that intervenes directly in the relationship of power, authority, and influence within the group. The change effort is directed at the work relationships among members; it is aimed at encouraging members to positively and productively change their roles. Role negotiation concentrates on objective assessment and deals solely with work-oriented issues. It is a systematic method for focusing attention on the many positive ways in which people can help one another. Because members decide what issues are to be addressed, this method is adjustable to the readiness level of the team to tackle tough issues. Through this method, team members gradually discover that they can achieve more for themselves through open negotiation than they can through isolated and competitive maneuvers; in time, the constructive process will replace the more restrictive and limiting one.

*Background.* In many organizations, the development of a human relations orientation among executives has led to an attempt to develop lines of communication, collaborative relationships based on mutual trust, and democratic decision-making processes with small groups. Another behavioral philosophy, oriented toward production and achievement, focuses on finding interests and tasks that develop the individual's abilities, creativity, and willingness to accept and exercise personal responsibility. Both of these popular approaches may be termed "tender-minded" in that they assume that people will be collaborative and productive if certain barriers are removed; they too easily dismiss factors such as competition, conflict, and the struggle for power. The problem of organizational change is often seen as releasing the human potential for collaboration and productivity, rather than countering greed, competitiveness, and exploitation. Organizational reality indicates that the actual forces affecting business executives do, in fact, include power seeking, influence peddling, intraorganizational politics, the withholding of information, manipulation, and dissension.

Few executives operate within an organizational world that is safe for openness, collaboration, creativity, and personal growth. Before executives can realize such an environment, they must first address the obstacles. As a useful tool in this confrontation, role negotiation is based on one elementary assumption: most people prefer a fairly negotiated settlement to a chaos of unresolved conflict. A modest but significant risk is expected from the participants, as they must be specific and candid about what changes in behavior, authority, and responsibility they wish to see brought about in others. If the participants take this risk, significant improvements in work effectiveness can usually be obtained.

*The Process Itself.* Often a third party, usually a skilled process consultant, is needed to work with the organizational group during the process of role clarification. If this is the case, the first step is to establish an understanding between team members and the consultant as to what they will expect from one another. For example, it is not the consultant's place to press people about their feelings; the focus should be on the mechanics and logistics of the work situation. How people feel about their work or about others in the group is their own business, and this information should be introduced only at the discretion of individual members. However, openness and honesty are expected and are essential for the achievement of results. The consultant should expect full disclosure about the work that people do, how they do it, and with whom they work; the consultant will ask members to be specific when expressing their expectations and demands in relation to the behaviors of others.

All agreements will finally be committed to writing. Negotiation relies heavily on the principle of quid pro quo, and the emphasis is on the positive aspects of mutual and equal exchange. Unfortunately, threats and pressures find their way into the negotiation process. There are numerous additional considerations and understandings that the group and consultant will need to work out prior to a full engagement in the role-negotiation process.

Once the group and consultant have reached an understanding about the overall work structure, it is time to focus on the decision-making and communication processes within the group, as these are the vehicles by which power and influence are exercised within an organization. To facilitate progress in these areas, members hold discussions and share information about the following questions: (1) Which activities should other members spend more time on or perform more effectively? (2) On which activities should other members spend less time? (3) Which activities enhance the productivity of the group and should be left alone? The members list and exchange their responses to these questions and conduct a clarification discussion, with a focus on channeling the collective energy generated by the sharing of demands and expectations toward successful problem solving and positive mutual influence, and away from potential conflicts.

After each member has had an opportunity to clarify the received information, the group selects issues for negotiation. This narrows down the issues into a manageable format that lends itself to exensive examination of particular issues. Members indicate areas where they want to exert influence and areas where they are willing to accept influence. The negotiation process consists of members extending contingent offers to one another in the form of "If you do $X$, I will do $Y$." Negotiation ends when all parties are satisfied that they will receive a reasonable return for whatever they agree to invest.

Next, the agreement is formalized in writing, and all participants sign the document. All agreements pertaining to individual members are reviewed by the whole group; this helps to test members' commitment, good faith, and reality orientation in relation to the agreements.

**Default.** Whenever any of the involved parties default on their end of an agreement, this must be discussed in depth by the entire group. During this open discussion, potential sanctions, pressures, and penalties can be considered and agreed on. Nonfulfillment of a bargain is an issue that must be thoroughly examined and successfully confronted.

**Follow-Up.** Once negotiation has been completed, it is a good idea to allow participants to operate within the terms of the initial agreements before further measures are introduced. One to three months after implementation, a review meeting should be held to renegotiate failed agreements and dispense with completed agreements. Outside influences and other variables with negative impacts can also be examined at this meeting. If the group has matured and grown into a more productive unit, new issues can be introduced for negotiation.

*Summary.* The concept of role negotiation is based on the assumption that people have truly individual and sometimes conflicting interests and that conflict and competition are naturally occurring elements in almost every situation. Since everyone looks out for his or her own interests to some extent, it is to be expected that individuals can at times be exploitative, distrustful, and overly competitive. An effective antidote for countering harmful competition and general mistrust is a negotiated settlement based on enforceable guarantees and mutual observance. The targets of change often include areas such as working relationships, duties, responsibilities, authority, and accountability. The forces that sustain positive change efforts stem from the ability and willingness of participants to administer or withhold rewards and sanctions in accordance with compliance or violation of negotiated agreements. Once people begin to deal with one another in this fashion, they will recognize the advantages for themselves and for the organization. This in turn leads to a more natural and genuine desire to maintain satisfying relationships that are built on openness, caring, and trust.

## Defining Responsibilities

Before a team can improve its effectiveness, it must decide how individual members' responsibilities for managing the team processes will be distributed. These responsibilities are frequently referred to as task responsibilities and maintenance responsibilities.

*Task Responsibilities.* These are the responsibilities that individual members need to take on for the team to sustain a concentrated effort in the direction of a specific task, and they include a number of specific roles within the group. The *initiator-contributor* proposes to the group new ideas or new angles regarding the group problem or goal: the adoption of a new group goal, the formation of a new definition of the problem, a method of handling a difficulty that the group has encountered, or a new manner of organizing the group for the task ahead. The *information seeker* asks for the clarification of suggestions to test their factual accuracy and adequacy in order to bring all pertinent facts to light so that the group can assess their validity and viability. The *opinion seeker,* on the other hand, asks for the clarification of values pertinent to the group's undertaking. The *information giver* offers facts or generalizations that vary in nature from authoritative and objective observation to opinions gleaned from personal experience. The *opinion giver* states beliefs or opinions concerning suggestions under consideration. As with the opinion seeker, the emphasis here is on the less tangible components, such as values or morale.

The *elaborator* first diagnoses and then presents the suggestions in a format that includes examples, developed meanings, rationales for and relationships of previous suggestions, and projections as to how well a suggestion might work if it were actually adopted by the group. The *coordinator* clarifies the relationships of various ideas and suggestions being considered and analyzes the interactions of various members and subgroups. The *orienter* defines the position of the group in relation to its goals, summarizing what has occurred, pointing out departures from agreements, and raising questions about the direction that the group is taking. The *evaluator-critic* examines the accomplishments of the group in the light of set standards that measure group functioning within the overall context of the group task, evaluating the practicality, logic, facts, and procedures of every suggestion. In an attempt to stimulate the group on to greater accomplishments, the *energizer* prods the group toward action and decisiveness. The *procedural technician* facilitates group movement by performing routine tasks: distributing materials, obtaining equipment, and so forth. The *recorder* (the "group memory") writes down all suggestions, maintains a record of group decisions, and keeps an outline of all discussions.

**Maintenance Responsibilities.** The *encourager* accepts, praises, and agrees with the contributions of others. He or she expresses warmth and solidarity with other group members, offers commendation and praise, and indicates an understanding and acceptance of other points of view, ideas, and suggestions. The *harmonizer* works to smooth out differences between members, attempts to reconcile disagreements, and strives to relieve tension. When a conflict involves personal ideas or positions, the *compromiser* tries to resolve the difficulties by admitting an error, administering some form of self-discipline, or simply meeting the others halfway on the disputed issue. The *gatekeeper/expediter* attempts to maintain communication channels by encouraging the participation of all members and by regulating the flow of discussion so that everyone has an opportunity to contribute. The *standard setter/ego ideal* attempts to lay out group norms that will lead to a more effective operation and establish standards that can be used to evaluate group performance. The *group observer/commentator* records various aspects of group processes and feeds this information, along with possible interpretations, back into the process of the group's evaluation of its own procedures. The *follower* floats along with the movement of the group, passively accepting the ideas of others and serving simply as an audience during group discussions.

# 6

# Setting Team and Individual Goals

A team of top managers in a large auto parts company was given the goal of landing the largest contract in the company's history: 90 percent of the business of the Chrysler Corporation. The team clearly knew its goals and how long it had to reach them. Each team member was clear about his or her role in making the sale. As a team, the group devised and implemented an action plan to win the contract. They impressed Chrysler and won the business.

As with roles and responsibilities, both individual and group goals must be clearly defined. When goals are clear, they act as tremendous motivators. In almost any organization that has experienced significant expansion and growth, the members of the organization express a high level of desire to achieve (McClelland and Winter, 1971). We also know that these desires are enhanced by the existence of clear and specific goals. When we adhere to the following principles, we are able to stimulate or maximize the desire to achieve.

- The specific goals of the job should be made explicit.
- Goals should represent a moderate degree of risk for the individuals involved.
- Goals can be adjusted as the situation warrants, especially when their odds of success are far below or above a fifty-fifty chance.
- Individuals should be given feedback in relation to their successes or failures in reaching goals.

- Rewards should be contingent on the achievement of goals.
- There should be a climate of mutual support, encouragement, and understanding.

These are relatively straightforward and simple guidelines for the establishment of individual goals. However, these goals must be established within the context of the team's objectives and goals. Managers often assign goals on a strictly individual basis rather than discussing them with the group as a whole, so that individuals have no idea of what other team members are trying to accomplish. When a manager does not strive to ensure that individual members clearly understand their roles, that manager is allowing work to compound into a maze of redundancy. There is considerable evidence that when the goal-setting process is conducted within the team format, teamwork is enhanced substantially and the likelihood that goals will be understood and enthusiastically undertaken is greatly increased.

The group goal-setting process can be illustrated by the following example. A team of managers in a large plastics manufacturing company met to discuss the general objectives and goals of their organization. The general manager of the division expressed an interest in getting members of the team involved in the goal-setting process, and they participated in establishing the general objectives. When the group had reached agreement on these objectives, the general manager announced that he would like the members of his team to think about how their personal objectives could fit into the general objectives and that he would like to meet with each member individually to discuss objectives and plans. This example is fairly typical of how many organizations approach the goal-setting process—as an exclusively one-on-one activity. Goals must be set on both an individual and a group level if teamwork is to be improved. With group goal setting, all members of the management team are present during the goal-setting process; although goals are set one person at a time, input is received from all members; and individuals take the initiative for establishing their own goals, while their superior offers support instead of immediate criticism.

## Individual Goal Setting

Individual goal setting typically proceeds according to the following pattern: The manager initiates goal setting by issuing a letter or directive announcing the program. Subordinate managers are encouraged to think about general goals for the organization and to fit their individual contributions into the overall goal-setting process. Individual members of the management team are then brought together for a discussion and eventual agreement on general goals, and relationship problems are handled. Individual members meet with their manager to negotiate goals. Goals are recorded, and a review period is established. When this period has passed, the manager reviews progress toward goals with the individual members, and new goals may be established.

Wendell French and Robert Hollmann (1973) mention a number of critical deficiencies in this approach, including the "likely long-range inadequacies of an autocratic form of 'Management by Objectives (MBO).'" (MBO is a management process of setting goals [objectives], developing plans for achieving the goals, and monitoring progress.) The one-on-one relationship does not deal with the interdependency of management positions within an organization. Without a doubt, any management organization is a highly interdependent system; that is, individuals are dependent on one another for the achievement of their objectives and goals. Since the accomplishment of each individual's task is contingent on separate tasks being completed by others, success is accelerated when these individual activities are coordinated into an overall effort that is unified and cohesive.

When individuals have not been fully informed as to how their separate tasks fit into the whole, a successful corporate effort is rendered much more difficult. Within the one-on-one process, the burden of coordinating objectives is placed on the individual. In addition, a manager's leadership style can dominate the one-on-one process, especially when that style is authoritative or autocratic. However, this process can sometimes lead managers to alter their styles. The one-on-one process can be riddled with communication gaps. Because individuals do not have information about what other members are doing, a negative form of competition tends to develop that inhibits collaboration and cooperation.

## Group Goal Setting

While the group goal-setting process is in some ways similar to individual goal setting, there are some important differences. With group goal setting, team members are asked in advance to think about their individual goals in relation to the team's goals, and then they meet to negotiate individual goals as a team. Every goal is shared with all members of the group, these goals are recorded, and review or goal-adjustment meetings are held when the situation warrants. The reviews may be conducted as group meetings but are usually held between an individual member and his or her superior, with the results shared among other members of the management team. All members of the management team attend regularly scheduled review meetings to diagnose and solve problems and establish new goals for the next period.

While the time required to assemble a group to set goals may make the process seem impractical, expending time on the front end of the goal-setting process will minimize confusion, conflict, and wasted effort. Group goal setting does, however, have some potential drawbacks. For instance, some managers might perceive the exchange of control involved as a loss of power or influence. It is sometimes difficult for a manager to accept the concept of sharing responsibility for the group's direction. Furthermore, because differences in competency are often clearly exposed during the group goal-setting process, people whose performance is deficient may feel threatened and embarrassed. However, such exposure may prompt other members of the team to help the person perform more effectively. Finally, because the development of collaborative and personal awareness skills is essential to the group goal-setting process, managers who have not studied the dynamics of teamwork may not be able to manage the process effectively.

Obviously, no one approach is perfect, and every process has limitations. Effective goal setting requires combining appropriate aspects of the different approaches into a viable program that matches the specific problem at hand.

## The Shifting of Power

"Every time people interact to influence the behavior in one another then power, as understood by the psychologist, is involved in their interaction. As we all interact with others in various formal and informal groups, we can witness the existence of power, how it tends to exert power, and the influence attempts of others to change our behavior. The very operation of the group involves a change of power" (Lawless, 1972, p. 231). "The most obvious way that a leader obtains power is through the organization which gives him the right to direct, evaluate, reward and punish within certain, rather well-defined limits. Within these boundaries a leader can expect the organization to support him. If an employee does not follow legitimate orders, the organization will administer disciplinary action or uphold the supervisor's right to discipline" (Chemers and Fiedler, 1974, p. 60).

When a manager is accustomed to exercising a certain amount of power through the group goal-setting process, it is often the manager's goals that are being stressed. In the one-on-one process, the manager shares equal power with the person sitting across the table. However, when the manager meets with a group of subordinates who clearly know that they are going to participate in the goal-setting process, the manager has released some of the control and power assigned by the organization (that is, certain responsibilities are delegated to subordinates). The critical element to the success of a group goal-setting process is the way in which power is delegated and shared. One of the reasons that group goal setting has become increasingly important is the fact that there has been a breakdown in the centralization of power throughout society as a whole. In Europe, particularly in West Germany and Sweden, a pervasive movement is under way in the direction of individual participation in overall management. This movement, called "codetermination," has spread at a rapid pace.

There are few explanations as to how or why the shift from a centralized power base to a distributive power base has taken place. Perhaps French's explanation would prove helpful: "a value frequently attributed to the applied behavioral scientists is a presumed value placed on democratization of organizations or on power equalization" (French and Bell, 1984, p. 52). French argues that behavioral scientists should play a major role in the process of shifting the power base from the central figures in an organization to the many individuals that actually make up the organization.

Recent studies have indicated that people in subordinate positions in an organization can carry significant weight in management decisions (Chemers and Fiedler, 1974). "Decentralization of power and control seems inevitable, given the conditions developing within the modern organization. Undoubtedly this will be a stumbling block to those grown accustomed to a traditionally heavy concentration in the leaders. Decentralization is even contrary to the Protestant ethic which calls for firm individual effort and striving. It calls, rather, for warmer and more human interaction and co-operation" (Lawless, 1972, p. 240). This point requires further attention. The basic problem inherent in group goal setting involves the manager's ability to adapt to the transference of power. David McClelland (Kolb, Rubin, and McIntyre, 1984, p. 180) has provided several insights into the "power-motive." "Since managers are primarily concerned with influencing others, it seems obvious that they should be characterized by a high need for power and that by studying the power motive we could learn something about the way effective managerial leaders work." Obviously, managers who are power-oriented will have difficulty transferring elements of control to other members of the team. Nonetheless, every manager can learn how to shift the responsibility for decision making and goal setting to members of the group without any loss of face and, perhaps, with an actual enhancement of power.

This process is illustrated by the experience of a manufacturing team that had been practicing MBO with rather

unproductive results. The team consisted of an area manager
and five plant managers. The area manager had been given the
appropriate resources and the approval of management to experiment with other approaches for establishing and achieving
goals. It was agreed that he would bring together his plant
managers for a series of three sessions: an introductory session
for the managers to reacquaint themselves with the concepts of
MBO; a goal-setting session, during which each plant manager
would negotiate directly with the area manager while other
members observed; and a review and planning session. The shift
from one-on-one goal setting to group goal setting took place
during the second session, where goals were negotiated. At the
end of the negotiation, the observing members filled out a questionnaire with their evaluations of the meeting. As this formal
feedback was presented, it became clear that some of the information would have been more useful had it been brought out
during the actual negotiation. After two rounds of one-on-one
negotiation, the area manager suggested that the observing
members should voice their comments whenever they thought
appropriate. It was at this point that the group goal-setting process began.

At the end of the second session, which lasted longer than
originally estimated, the area manager asked for overall feedback on the group goal-setting process. Unanimously, members
of the group expressed an interest in and satisfaction with this
approach. The area manager, not totally satisfied, suggested
that they reflect further on this process and write him letters
expressing their viewpoints by the end of three weeks. This was
done; all the members still felt that this was the best way to
negotiate goals. Therefore, it was decided that the goal review
and planning session that was to be held six months later would
be conducted on a group basis. At that session, the area manager
maintained a relatively low profile, and the plant managers
worked supportively together to help each other accomplish objectives. All further goal-setting and review meetings were then
designed to be conducted on a group basis.

Clearly, a shift from the one-on-one process to the group
goal-setting process can alter the behavior of the members of

a group. The list below presents some of the changes that occur through this process.

| One-on-One Process | Group Process |
|---|---|
| Boss initiates the process. | Individual initiates process. |
| Boss talks 50 percent of the time. | Boss talks 20–30 percent of the time. |
| Employee reacts to boss's questions. | Employee and group react to questions. |
| Suggestions are made by employee. | Suggestions are made by the group. |
| Boss supports the employee. | Group and boss support the individual. |
| Process observation skills are low. | Process observation skills are high. |

Other observable signs that can accompany a shift in power include an increased sensitivity to the creativity and spontaneity of the group, an increased sense of commitment to the accomplishment of goals, an increased satisfaction with overall results, and a more attentive boss who is concerned with gathering significant input from all members. The benefits resulting from these changes include better communication among group members, better diagnosis and problem solving, improved generation of ideas and solutions to problems, greater support among members of the team, higher trust levels among members of the team, more overall teamwork, and higher performance achievement.

As our society moves in the direction of a more involving and participative approach to living, managers can expect that employees will want and insist on more involvement in management activities. With this in mind, managers will need to become more aware of the value and energy that result from the inclusion of an entire group.

# 7

## Improving Team Member Relationships

Managing interpersonal relationships among team members is one of the most important aspects of teamwork. Interpersonal relationships act as the lubricant does in an engine. Without attention to the way people work together, teams can overheat and teamwork can break down. Interpersonal relationships have to do with how people react to each other in terms of ideas, tasks, and emotions. Thinking and action are closely related to the way a person feels. If a person presents an idea that he or she feels is a good one, and that idea is criticized, that person would probably react in a way expressive of feelings: with defensiveness or anger. Whatever people do is almost always linked to their feelings. This chapter begins with a general discussion of interpersonal competence and then presents ways to manage the ever-present problem of interpersonal conflict.

### Interpersonal Competence

Managers and supervisors continually make statements and ask questions like the following: "Why don't my team members work together?" "I've talked to them, but it doesn't seem to help." "Their work is all right, but they must get along with each other." "Sure they're competent, but they don't show any initiative to work with others." Such problems, and hundreds more, reflect the most painful task of those who have direct responsibility for teams. Bringing about a change in individual team member behavior is not easy. We all desire to be more competent when it comes to influencing other people; it is not surprising, however, that we all more or less miss the target. Most people know what it means to be technically competent—to have mastered certain skills and subject matter necessary to perform the "nonpersonal" aspects of their positions. But few know how to be really effective in dealing with others—that is, to be interpersonally competent.

Typical manifestations of interpersonal incompetence include restricted commitment, gamesmanship, and deceptive and out-of-character behavior. One of the most serious consequences of this incompetence is people's lack of awareness of their own behavior patterns and their impact on others. Another is lack of awareness by managers of their subordinates' negative feelings and how they hinder team performance. Probably the most significant consequence of interpersonal incompetence is the distrust and antagonism that it fosters among team members. Distrust grows out of the secretiveness of managers and their failure to share ideas and information. Such distrust and antagonism are rarely displayed openly; they are most commonly manifested at critical decision points in the form of resistance. Trust, on the other hand, can be illustrated as in Figure 2.

Interpersonal competence is shown in the ability to cope effectively with interpersonal relationships. There are three key factors in effective coping:

1.  The situation must be perceived accurately, and the relevant information must be identified. Interpersonal information is as important as technical information.
2.  Problems must be solved in such a way that they remain solved. A common supervisory frustration results from forcing a problem to solution today, only to have it reappear tomorrow.
3.  The solution reached must not lead to a deterioration in supervisory-subordinate working relations. For example, if a problem is solved in such a way that the superior loses confidence in an employee or the employee is left resentful, the relationship between them has been damaged, and this will lead to future difficulties.

Figure 2. The Trust Cycle.

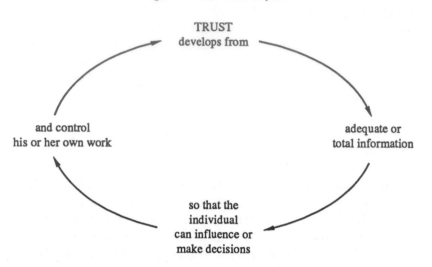

Through observation and research conducted with hundreds of teams, Chris Argyris (1971) of Harvard University has identified some of the key behaviors and norms that foster effective interpersonal relationships. These are shown in Table 1.

## Managing Interpersonal Conflict

One of the most common team problems is ineffective management of interpersonal relationships, which often leads to conflict between members. For example, a large energy company had been conducting team-building sessions for several years, using a seminar format as well as working within the team structure itself. The training had covered a number of activities focused on improving team functioning, with repeated emphasis on the importance of conflict resolution and minimizing the negative impact of conflict among team members. But the company found no clear evidence that the training had helped teams to become any more efficient at managing differences among members: in almost all cases, teams showed no substantial improvement in the way they managed conflict, and conflict remained the number-one problem for most of them.

Disagreement exists whenever activities are incompatible. An action (including thought) is incompatible with another when it prevents, obstructs, interferes with, or injures another's action, making it less likely or less effective. Although most managers are aware of disagreements and have received training in conflict resolution, they seldom seem to assign a high priority to solving conflict problems. The reality is that excessive conflict on teams can become an insidious problem that can eat away at cohesiveness, cooperation, and trust.

Conflict grows out of power differences, scarcity of resources, and social and value differences. It manifests in two basic forms: antagonistic psychological relations and antagonistic interactions. The former can be described in terms of incompatible goals, mutually exclusive interests, emotional hostility, and differieng value structures; the latter are more overt and can range from subtle, indirect, and highly controlled forms of interference to direct, violent, and uncontrollable struggles. Conflict can arise from numerous sources within a team setting, and managers and team members must understand its unpredictability.

Many sociologists, psychologists, and theorists view differences and the resulting conflicts as a disease to be stamped out, and literature on conflict is laced with words such as *stress, strain,* and *fight.* It is no wonder that conflict and disagreement are generally viewed negatively. To operate effectively, however, groups require both harmony and disharmony. If the team leader and members understand how to do it, disagreement and differences can be turned to the advantage of a team so that the differences that do arise are no longer viewed as intolerable or destructive and can even result in benefits for a team.

When conflict is suppressed, long-standing differences can often reduce the effectiveness of a team. If differences are brought to the surface, however, they can be dealt with and the problem resolved, which tends to increase the cohesiveness and effectiveness of the team. Because it stimulates interest and energy, conflict often fosters creativity and intensity among team members. Bringing differences to the surface can also result in better ideas and more innovative solutions. Better decisions are

Table 1. Dimensions of Interpersonal Competence.

| | Positive | Negative |
|---|---|---|
| Individual behavior | Experimenting—examining ideas or feelings to disclose new aspects of them; being willing to test ideas and feelings through actual experience: "Let's give it a try and see what happens." "I'm willing to try this, although I've never done it before." | Rejecting experiment—not examining ideas or feelings to make new discoveries; being unwilling to subject ideas or feelings to a test: "What's wrong with the way we're doing it?" "There's no sense continuing this, because you're wrong." |
| | Openness—being receptive to new information, ideas, and feelings from oneself and others; being willing to ask questions, to consider new facts and feelings, to put oneself in others' shoes: "Please tell me more about that." "I'm not sure I understand you." "I didn't realize I felt so strongly about that." "I wonder why I've never seen that before." | Lack of openness—being unreceptive to new ideas and feelings from oneself and others: "Don't bother me with the facts. My mind is made up." "I'm sure I'm right. Let's get on with it." |
| | Owning—the willingness to take public responsibility for (that is, ownership of) an idea or feeling; to "own up"; "I believe that. . . ." "In my opinion, we should talk. . . ." "I do not agree with you." | Not owning—being unwilling to take responsibility for ideas or feelings: "I am not upset" (although flustered and red-faced). "I don't mind being misunderstood" (or unappreciated). "I don't care. It's up to you." "I didn't say that!" |

| | | |
|---|---|---|
| Interpersonal behavior | *Helping others to experiment*—"If I understand you correctly, you are suggesting...." "How can I help you...?" | *Not helping others to experiment*—"This is crazy. Why don't you forget about it?" "For your sake, let's drop it. If you don't it's going to upset the group." "You know where that's going to lead, don't you?" |
| | *Helping others to be open*—"Let's explore that a little further." "Would it help to consider the following ideas?" "I can understand your feeling that way." | *Not helping others to be open*—"You'd be a fool to listen to him." "Why do you spend time raising these issues?" |
| | *Helping others to own*—"If I understand you correctly, you are suggesting...." "Bill has a point that we ought to help him get across to us." | *Not helping others to own*—influencing others not to own; interrupting: "You do have a problem." "I hope you don't mean what you're saying." |
| Social norms | *Trust*—the ability to risk oneself in a relationship. | *Mistrust* |
| | *Concern*—interest in the ideas and feelings of self and others; curiosity about and encouragement of others. | *Antagonism*—being unmindful of or unconcerned about others; being hostile toward oneself and others; being judgmental and disapproving. |
| | *Individuality*—valuing the expression of individual ideas or feelings; supporting personal independence by encouraging people to act according to the way they think and feel. | *Conformity*—limiting choices, requiring dependence on others, blind following and stagnation. |

reached when people share their points of view and bring them together through a consensus approach. Finally, when team members begin to air their differences in a constructive way, they also develop their articulation and argument skills and learn how to extract precise meanings from the information they receive.

These potential benefits of conflict are frequently overlooked because of the negative connotations of the word *conflict*. The negative images of conflict must be overcome if teams are to utilize its positive side.

*Sources of Disagreements.* Conflict often begins unobtrusively and seemingly inconsequentially, such as with a simple argument between two team members. Given the volatility of human nature, however, disagreement seldom goes unnoticed. People frequently sit and stew over disagreements and automatically react when similar situations arise. When conflict remains unchecked, people may either blow up or clam up; as conflict continues, they begin to entrench themselves in certain positions and develop arguments that affirm their posture. As conflict persists and becomes more acute, people eventually try to avoid it, so that the source of the conflict is never effectively dealt with. When emotions are high and the parties involved have decided to take retaliatory actions whenever the opportunity presents itself, conflict will continue and will be compounded. In some cases, retaliation takes on the form of sabotage, with people maliciously planning to find some way to get back at their opponent. Such conflict can eventually lead to serious consequences, ranging from complete withdrawal to physical violence.

Within a large health care organization, a case of unhealthy conflict eventually led two high-level officers to completely avoid one another. The conflict stemmed from a series of meetings between a man and a woman who were officers at the same level of the organization. The man had expressed dissatisfaction with how the woman had conducted herself in completing a reporting process. She reacted negatively to this criticism, and he arrogantly went on about his business. Thereafter, similar incidents arose between them until during one encounter, complete with yelling and finger-pointing (each person unshakably convinced that the other was wrong), the one officer referred to the other as a "dumb woman." At this point the conversation ended. This conflict was not revealed until two years later, during a team-building exercise. During these two years, neither officer had directly spoken to or written memos to the other; all communication between them had been processed through the president of the organization. The situation was finally exposed when, during the team-building session, one of the combatants requested that the president serve as the exchange point of all their communications. The president apparently had grown accustomed to this unusual method of communication and had not questioned it. However, once it was brought out, the two combatants finally acknowledged the origins of their disagreement, its evolution, and the point at which they had decided to let it continue unchecked. Because these two people held high positions, the effects of their conflict had serious reverberations throughout the entire organization.

Exposing the sources of conflict is not an easy task. It is difficult to bring combative parties to a table to talk about their differences when anger and emotions are running high. However, when conflict is detected in its early stages, it is much easier to manage.

The primary sources of disagreement in the team setting generally fall into the categories of communication factors, structural factors, and personal factors. Communication factors are among the most important. As the average American spends 70 percent of his or her waking hours involved in some form of communication (writing, reading, speaking, or listening), barriers to communication can be a major source of misunderstanding. Such barriers include insufficient exchange of information, semantic difficulties (words meaning different things to different people), receivers hearing only what is to their liking, sender and receiver having different perceptions, nonverbal cues being ignored, and sender or receiver being emotionally upset. Structural factors include the size of the organization, length of service (turnover rate), participation levels, reward systems, power and the ability to influence others, and interdependence.

Personal factors include self-esteem, job satisfaction, personal goals, values, and needs.

***Conflict Resolution.*** Once the origin of conflict has been identified, divergent opinions and emotions can be more accurately examined and understood. Obviously, when the range of potential responses to disagreement is understood, conflict itself can be more effectively managed. A rough approximation of this range is presented in Figure 3 (Stepsis, 1974). The most common

Figure 3. Conflict Responses.

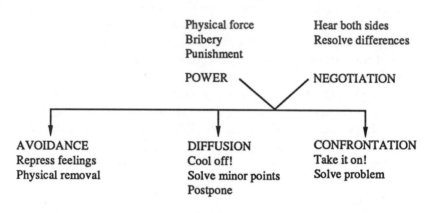

response to open conflict is avoidance; for example, two parties walk away from each other and refrain from any further engagement. Avoidance indicates that disagreement has developed into destructive conflict. People often think that to diffuse a situation is the appropriate response, because it gives the two parties a chance to cool down and postpone facing up to their disagreement until they are able to come together and discuss their differences rationally. Unfortunately, diffusion does not adequately deal with the emotions involved in conflict. These emotions are only temporarily suppressed and will eventually resurface. Another response to significant conflict is confrontation. Sometimes individuals are encouraged to go toe-to-toe with each other in a struggle to resolve their differences. Sometimes the leader of the team adopts a position of power and simply threatens the conflicting parties with punishment if they do not resolve their differences. Sometimes bribery is used: "If you do what I ask, I'll give you this." In extreme cases, even physical force is brought into play. But these approaches can be very costly, and they rarely improve the way the team functions.

The most effective response to conflict is negotiation, which offers flexibility and viability that the other responses lack. The negotiation process involves listening to both sides, seeking out common areas of interest and agreement, and building on common agreements so that individuals can understand each other's points of view. To effectively resolve disagreement through the negotiation process, team leaders must learn and apply four essential skills: diagnosis, initiation, listening, and problem solving.

- *Diagnosis.* The team leader must be adept at analyzing contrasting points of view and skilled at helping the involved parties recognize areas of common understanding, as well as points of difference. An accurate diagnosis can be the key to unlocking the sources of conflict.
- *Initiation.* Any team leader who hopes to resolve conflict must take the initiative by bringing the disagreement to the surface as soon as it is apparent and dealing with the range of responses to conflict.
- *Listening.* To effectively resolve differences between individuals, the team leader must be a good listener, able to hear the emotional aspects of what is being said. The leader must understand messages with empathy and convey this understanding to those who have shared the information.
- *Problem Solving.* There are numerous steps in the problem-solving process: gathering data, both positive and negative; looking at the impact of the data on the parties involved; examining alternative approaches for bridging differences; identifying which solution will work most effectively; and developing an action plan, compatible with the involved parties, that will ultimately resolve the conflict.

A conflict between two parties is most likely to be productively resolved through the negotiation process if both parties stand to gain something from the resolution, if they each have some power in the situation (that is, the ability to reward or sanction the other), and if there is interdependency between the two parties—they need each other to do their jobs. To resolve their disagreements, the parties are brought together and asked the following questions:

1.  What is the problem as you perceive it?
2.  What does the other person do that contributes to the problem?
3.  What do you want or need from the other person?
4.  What do you do that contributes to the problem?
5.  What first step can you take to resolve the problem?

Each party is questioned while the other listens, asking questions only for clarification. After the questioning, the parties enter a discussion to arrive at a mutual definition and understanding of the problem. This process should offer the parties an opportunity to vent and blame—to get hostility out of their systems. For the process to be effective, both parties should be willing to admit partial responsibility for the problem. Good listening, low defensiveness, and an ability to stay in a problem-solving mode are also important. Sometimes a third party can help with this.

Finally, the parties reach agreement on steps to resolve the problem. Such agreements are most effective if they offer some sort of quid pro quo and if they ensure that cooperation is necessary for both parties' survival. Agreements and action steps should be put in writing as the negotiation proceeds to prevent problems from being quickly glossed over and to reduce the chances of a misunderstanding at a later point.

## Summary

Once the sources of conflict have been revealed, people are usually able to understand the actual facts of the case and from this mutual understanding reach an agreement. Once areas of agreement are identified, individual parties can look for ways to bridge the gap between their way of thinking and that of the other person, arrive at a consensus, and develop a process for resolving problems in the future. The key to this process is exposing the different positions as early as possible. The longer conflict persists, the more difficult it is to manage; once conflict has evolved into open warfare and sabotage, it is very difficult to resolve.

Although conflict is a common problem in teams, it should not be viewed in a purely negative light. When properly managed, disagreements provide an opportunity for differences between people to be resolved to the advantage of the team. The way an individual responds to other people has a direct relationship to the way other people respond to that individual. Being able to distinguish between positive and negative responses can be a valuable tool in improving interpersonal relationships.

# ❦ 8 ❦

# Making Decisions and Solving Problems in Teams

Robert Townsend (1970), former president of Avis Car Rental, stands behind the traditional wisdom that says that two heads are better than one. He has demonstrated a clear understanding of the value of "groupthink" in decision making and problem solving. Townsend learned through experience that when he makes decisions individually his rate of success tends to be slightly better than 50 percent, but when the creative, idea-generating power of his staff is added to the process, the rate of success greatly increases. Obvious advantages of a group decision-making and problem-solving process are that it expands the range of available options, enhances the quality of the solutions, and increases commitment among those involved. However, any group problem-solving or decision-making process takes more time than do individual-based processes. This question is always faced by active managers: "Should I invest the time in working it through my group, or should I get on with it?" Most often, the best answer is to work it through with the group. To gain the advantages of "groupthink," managers must learn how to productively direct the processes that affect group actions, attitudes, and decisions.

## Team Problem Solving

One of the first things that a manager does when considering the problem-solving process is to look for signs that indicate a need to switch from individual to collective problem solving. Following are some of the typical symptoms that signal the need for this change:

1.  A limited number of alternatives and courses of action are generated outside the context of the team.
2.  Frequently, though an immediate problem is solved, the solution itself creates new problems.
3.  The underlying problem is not really solved but is given only a cosmetic treatment. Such a treatment may ease the discomfort or pain connected with the problem, but it does not solve the problem.
4.  Individual problem solvers are frequently heard to lament, "Oh, why didn't I think of that" or "It's too late now, I should have thought of it earlier." When only one person is involved, too many considerations are discovered in hindsight.
5.  Individual problem solvers tend to jump from early symptoms of the problem directly to the solution; such solutions usually do not work over the long haul.

An example of impatient problem solving occurred in a large manufacturing plant in a small Ohio town. The plant manager decided to eliminate two of the plant's four copying machines because he felt that employees were misusing the "privilege" of having copying machines in various locations. He kept one machine near his own office and one out in the plant. The net result of this change was that people got tied up in long lines while trying to use the copier near his office. This frustrated the plant manager, as well as his secretary, and an excessive amount of time was consumed in waiting to get to the equipment. This manager's hasty decision to solve the problem without first investigating the questions of utilization, need, and location led to a larger problem than the one he started out with. Eventually, the two additional machines returned.

A logical problem-solving process generally includes the following steps:

- *Define the problem:* Identify, locate, and describe as precisely as possible the obstacles or conditions that stand in the way of achieving objectives or cause undesirable performance or behavior.
- *Clarify relevant objectives:* Review and restate the short- and long-term outcomes to be achieved in relation to the problem, addressing both departmental and institutional goals.
- *Generate alternatives:* Develop a list of possible actions to achieve the desire objectives. Consider possible causes of the problem.
- *Develop action plan:* Determine the preferred alternative. Assign action steps to appropriate individuals. Predict problems likely to occur and what will be done. Inform all those involved of the plan.
- *Implement:* Initiate action to achieve the desired objective and to sustain the desired consequences.
- *Follow up:* Initiate feedback measures to ensure that actions were carried out as intended. Monitor status of possible adverse side-effects of actions.

These steps reflect the problem-solving process that is generally used in science, engineering, and other formal disciplines. What is different about this process in the organizational context is the involvement of a group. In order to properly define a problem, clarify relative objectives, generate action plans, implement, and follow up, input is required from all members of the group. Patience and care need to be exercised to ensure that all team members are participating and that their ideas are heard and utilized. Otherwise, members of the group will hold back, refusing to build on the ideas of other members, and not be supportive of a solution.

A constant theme runs through any group problem-solving process: whenever people are interacting, they tend to take the easy way out if faced with a difficult problem. Given the options of facing up to differences of opinion, planning ahead, working out some kind of group task, or avoiding problems altogether, group members can be expected to choose the alternative of avoidance unless the team leader plays an active role in ensuring that they remain committed to the process. No one knows exactly why people tend to take the easy way out, or why they avoid dealing directly with a problem, but there are numerous practical techniques that can be used to alleviate this problem. These techniques include planning in advance, having a clear agenda, scheduling meetings at times that are convenient for members of the group, making sure that agreements are recorded, and managing the communication process. Most people seem to have mixed feelings about group participation: on the one hand, the desire to be involved and to have a say in what is being done, and on the other, a tendency to avoid expressing a point of view for fear of the consequences. Managers must learn to take advantage of the former and minimize the latter. This can be done through careful planning of meetings and active management of the process, with a high level of sensitivity to the participants.

## Team Decision Making

Team decision making is a carefully designed process that makes certain all members of the team are on board when each decision is finally made. Managers can improve the effectiveness of group decision making by establishing a cooperative rather than a competitive group environment, one in which people feel like assisting as opposed to competing with one another. A high level of cohesiveness is also necessary for effective group decision making. However, cohesiveness is a tricky condition to establish, and it rarely comes about easily. Cohesiveness is built on trust and confidence among team members, and this requires that the behavior of each team member convey supportiveness and a willingness to help other members of the team.

The benefits of group cohesiveness are illustrated by the experiences of a team of five plant managers and their district manager who came together to establish group goals. They did an excellent job of establishing goals for their plants, sharing in the goal-setting process, helping one another, and generally supporting each other's goals. When they later met for a review session, however, one of the plant managers expressed great concern about problems he was having in meeting his goals. Though the district manager had doubts about the struggling plant manager's ability to solve his problems, two members of the team who had previously been managers in the plant stepped forward and offered to assist the troubled plant manager, who accepted their offer without hesitation. With their combined experience, they found a solution that worked.

The ability of a team to make group decisions is closely related to the personalities of the people on the team, as well as to the task at hand. If the members of the team are cooperative and noncompetitive and the task requires multiple disciplines and the sharing of responsibility, the group decision-making process should flow smoothly. Although not all team environments are positive, managers must always encourage members to develop productive attitudes and postures as cooperative participants in the group decision-making process.

A number of methods can be used to facilitate the group decision-making process. Brainstorming is a method that generates imaginative and creative solutions to a problem. With this method, members are encouraged to come up with extreme and, in some cases, outlandish methods for solving the problem. They are encouraged to build on one another's ideas; criticism of any generated idea is forbidden. Through this process, members see their individual contributions entering into the decision-making process and thus tend to be more accepting of the final decision.

The Delphi process uses a somewhat different method. Each member independently and anonymously writes down comments and suggestions about ways to deal with the problem, which are then compiled, reproduced, and distributed to the team members for observation and reaction. Each member provides feedback to the entire group concerning each of the comments and proposed solutions. Finally, the members reach consensus on which solution is most acceptable to the group as a whole. The obvious benefit of this kind of process is that it allows team members to see where their ideas are being included in the final decision.

With the nominal group technique, each member of the team is given a written problem to be solved and orally presents his or her ideas about solving the problem to the total group. Next, each member discusses each idea, clarifying and elaborating on it and providing feedback and evaluation. Finally, members independently and anonymously rank the ideas, and a group decision is reached as to which ideas have the highest accurate ranking.

All of these methods focus on reaching group decisions through consensus. Decision making through consensus means that all members of a group are provided an opportunity to present their views, and then all accept the group decision. Consensus requires careful extracting and recording of ideas from all participants so that everyone's ideas are considered in reaching the decision and, therefore, everyone can support that decision.

Gordon Lippitt (1978) offers some valuable advice on the subject of team decision making. He outlines eight important criteria for an effective process:

1. A clear definition of the problem.
2. A clear understanding of who has the responsibility for the decision.
3. Effective communication for idea production.
4. Appropriate size of group for decision making.
5. A means for effective testing of different alternatives.
6. A method for building commitment to the decision.
7. Honest commitment of the leader to the group decision-making process.
8. Agreement on the procedures and methods for decision making prior to deliberation on the issue.

This chapter concludes with two practice exercises to assist managers in learning how to manage group problem-solving and decision-making processes (Francis and Young, 1979). Exhibit 6 involves the use of an effective problem-solving survey designed to identify the strengths and weaknesses of the team problem-solving process. Exhibit 7 concerns decision making within the group context. These two exercises can serve as a starting point for a discussion of group problem solving and decision making.

## Exhibit 6. Effective Problem-Solving Survey.

*Purpose:* to identify strengths and weaknesses in team problem solving; to set agendas for strengthening the weakest characteristics.

*Time:* Forty-five minutes.

*Materials:* one copy of the Effective Problem-Solving Survey for each participant; a large newsprint pad and felt-tipped markers or a chalkboard and chalk; blank paper and a pencil for each participant.

*Method:*

I.   The leader distributes one copy of the Effective Problem-Solving Survey, paper, and a pencil to each member and tells the members to read the instructions and complete the survey (five minutes).

II.  After the survey has been completed, the leader asks whether the participants want to report their individual scores orally or write them down and turn them in anonymously.

III. The leader collects the scores, charts them, and identifies the two items with the lowest scores (ten minutes).

IV.  The members discuss the problem items and identify six action steps that could help the group improve in these two areas. The leader charts the suggestions and makes them available for reference at the next working session (thirty minutes).

### Effective Problem-Solving Survey

Instructions: Please give your candid opinion of your team's most recent problem-solving session by rating its characteristics on the seven-point scales shown below. Circle the appropriate number on each scale to represent your evaluation.

| | | |
|---|---|---|
| Lacking order and poorly controlled | 1 2 3 4 5 6 7 | Orderly and well controlled |
| Confusion about objectives | 1 2 3 4 5 6 7 | Clear and shared objectives |
| Organization inappropriate to task | 1 2 3 4 5 6 7 | Organization flexible, appropriate to task |
| Criteria for success not established | 1 2 3 4 5 6 7 | Clear criteria for success |
| Information poorly evaluated | 1 2 3 4 5 6 7 | Information well analyzed |
| Planning inadequate | 1 2 3 4 5 6 7 | Planning effective, thorough |
| Action ineffective | 1 2 3 4 5 6 7 | Action effective, adequate |
| No attempt to learn from the experience | 1 2 3 4 5 6 7 | Thorough review to help team learn from experience |
| Time wasted | 1 2 3 4 5 6 7 | Time well used |
| People withdrew or became negative | 1 2 3 4 5 6 7 | Everyone participated positively |

## Exhibit 7. Decision-Making Survey.

*Purpose:* to examine how the team and individual members typically make decisions; to plan changes in the team's decision-making process.

*Time:* one hour or more.

*Materials:* a copy each of the Decision-Making Checklist and the Decision-Making Interpretation Chart and a pencil for each participant; a large newsprint pad and felt-tipped markers or chalkboard and chalk.

*Background:* One of the most important questions regarding decision making is "Who actually decides?" From answers to this question, five different types of decision making can be clearly identified:

1. *Individual decisions.* One person, usually the boss, actually makes a decision, and others who are involved in the situation are expected to abide by it.

2. *Minority decisions.* A few of those involved in a situation meet to consider the matter and make a decision, and this is binding for all concerned.

3. *Majority decisions.* More than half of those involved in a situation make a decision, and this is binding for all concerned. Many political and democratic organizations use this principle.

4. *Consensus decisions.* An entire group considers a problem on the basis of reason and discussion. Each member expresses a view, and a decision is made as to which direction all members can commit themselves to, at least in part.

5. *Unanimous decisions.* Each person fully agrees on the action to be taken, and everyone concerned can fully subscribe to the decision taken.

People are much more likely to be committed to a decision if they have been involved in making it than if some other person or small group has made it on their behalf. Therefore, involving more people in the decision-making process increases commitment, although it also increases the difficulty of coming to an agreement.

*Method:*

I. The leader introduces the activity using the background information provided here.

II. The leader gives each participant a copy of the Decision-Making Checklist and the Decision-Making Interpretation Chart.

III. The participants complete the Decision-Making Interpretation Chart.

IV. The leader instructs each participant to choose the style of decision-making that he or she prefers for team meetings and then to share this choice with the group, giving brief reasons for the preference.

V. While the preferences are presented, the leader charts them on the newsprint pad, showing their frequency and rank order.

VI. The leader directs the participants to choose a decision-making style for their team. If there are differences among the individual preferences, the team works to resolve them and to reach a decision on an appropriate style. When the decision has been made, the team identifies the style by which it was reached. Then the team works to identify three or more actions that could be taken in the next meeting to ensure that the chosen style will succeed. If there is unanimity about the preferred style, the team identifies three or more actions that can be taken in the next meeting to ensure that the preferred style will work.

Exhibit 7. Decision-Making Survey, Cont'd.

### Decision-Making Checklist

*Instructions:* Think about your typical ways of making decisions, then read each of the statements below and choose five that are most typical for you. When you have completed your selection, refer to the Decision-Making Interpretation Chart.

1. When decision making is necessary, a few of us usually get together and take care of it.
2. The senior person usually decides, and that is it.
3. People really get a chance to express their views.
4. Typically, everyone agrees somewhat with the decisions taken.
5. We frequently decide on the basis of majority decisions.
6. One person is in charge and effectually makes decisions.
7. Everyone often freely agrees with decisions and supports them wholeheartedly.
8. There is a small clique that runs things around here.
9. Decisions are made when people decide on a particular course of action.
10. We would not make a decision until everyone is completely in agreement.
11. People are free to air their views, but the boss decides.
12. A few people usually dominate the group.
13. Decisions are not made unless everyone can accept proposals to some extent.
14. A numerical majority is required before decisions are made.
15. Each member actively supports decisions.

### Decision-Making Interpretation Chart

After you have marked five statements, circle the statement numbers in the first column shown below, then total each row. The highest scores represent the typical decision-making styles of your group.

| Statement Numbers | Totals | Style |
|---|---|---|
| 2 - 6 - 11 | | Individual dominance |
| 1 - 8 - 12 | | Minority influence |
| 5 - 9 - 14 | | Majority democracy |
| 3 - 4 - 13 | | Consensus |
| 7 - 10 - 15 | | Unanimous view |

## ♣ 9 ♣

# Developing Effective
# Team Leadership

The following dialogue between a manager and four subordinates is fairly typical of the way many managers conduct a staff meeting. Examine how this team functions during the interchange between members and to what degree the manager receives the kind of cooperation and support he needs to effectively run his organization.

*Mr. M:*  Good morning! I'm sorry to be a little bit late. Well, I think that you have all had plenty of time to look over the reorganization plan. I want constructive comments from all of you. The plan isn't perfect. What plan is? But a hell of a lot of thought has gone into it. Julia, what are your thoughts?

*Ms. A:*  It's intelligently thought out. It's got lots of possibilities.

*Mr. M:*  Yes, but what are the problems? That's what I need to hear from all of you.

*Ms. A:*  Well, in my division, it will do fine. I mean it depends on inspection. If my team goes for it, they will follow through.

*Mr. M:*  Is there any reason why they should? Do you think they won't, Julia? I want your thinking on that.

*Ms. A:*  Well, the change involves more than one department.

*Mr. M:*  I tried to arrange it so that every department meshes. I think that you can see that.

*Ms. A:*    That's quite clear. If everything works out, I think that we might even beat our quota.

*Mr. M:*    Good! Bill, how about you? You're very good at spotting any weakness a plan might have. What do you see?

*Mr. B:*    Well, I was wondering what will happen when the raw stock comes in. The new high-speed machines won't get here for another year.

*Mr. M:*    Right, I knew you would spot that one. If you'll turn to page six of the plan, I think that is provided for there, isn't it? In the double-shift system.

*Mr. B:*    Sure, there it is. I think that my department will benefit a lot from the changes. No doubt about it.

*Mr. M:*    Dan, what roadblocks do you see for your people here?

*Mr. C:*    None at all! The figures look reasonable to me.

*Mr. M:*    Rebecca, how about you?

*Ms. D:*    As far as I can see, the whole plan looks well conceived, and any bugs could be ironed out very easily.

*Mr. M:*    I am grateful to all of you. You know how I am, and you know how we work here. I wouldn't want to commit us to anything that we really couldn't live with or that wouldn't improve the performance in each of our departments.

Thousands of similar meetings occur every day in almost every organization throughout this country. While the manager in this case performed his function as a manager, what approach did he use to get the job accomplished? Remember, he was attempting to develop a whole new operation, and he wanted support and input from his team members. Did he in fact obtain this support? Was he able to get ideas and contributions from this team? It does not appear that he was. Therefore, we will examine what the manager was doing that affected the way the meeting turned out.

The manager in this case took the power position and directed questions one at a time to each of his subordinates. These questions were directive in nature, as well as limiting in terms of the kind of response that the manager expected. All the responses he received were guarded and cautious. When subordinates did begin to speak up, the manager countered that he had anticipated their points and that they were already covered in the plan. This behavior, typical of many managers, does not facilitate getting the best out of the total group. Such behavior is not problem-oriented, nor does it demonstrate a smooth flow of information or a sharing of ideas. In simple terms, this manager is not a facilitative manager, and he probably lacks any real awareness of the facilitative skills that are required to get the best out of his team.

If a facilitative approach to the same problem were used by this manager, the results might resemble the following:

*Mr. M:*    Good morning! Sorry to be a little bit late. By this time you should all have had a chance to read the proposal that was sent to you several days ago. I want to be clear that the purpose of this meeting is to get your input and ideas to make sure that this proposal does not overlook any areas or problems that are central to making the entire plan work. What I would like to suggest is that you each take a few minutes to explain your thoughts on the subject, and then we'll compare the information and relate it back to the proposal. Is there anyone who would like to start off the discussion? Yes, Julia, why don't you go ahead.

*Ms. A:*    I believe it is a well-designed proposal, and, as you know, we have been over parts of it in the previous discussions. I'm quite certain that if we can iron out the final bugs, it will work well for us. It is my belief that we may have a problem with inspection—that we may not have enough inspectors for the speed of the operation that we are proposing. I'd like to examine this problem with the group.

*Mr. M:*   I think that falls into Bill's area. Could we have your comments on this, Bill?

*Mr. B:*   As I believe I mentioned previously, I was a bit concerned about this also. However, considering how we have organized our staff, it looks like we could shift some people over from Line B to this new operation, once it's in gear. In any event, I would like to try it, using the current staff and without expanding at this point. I would, however, like to have the option of being able to open it up for future discussion if we find we can't meet the needs under the new plan.

*Mr. M:*   Are there any other comments or thoughts on this point? Yes, Bob.

*Mr. C:*   I think we ought not to run the risk of finding ourselves shorthanded when it comes to inspection. We ought to develop our contingency plan at this point so that when the time comes, we don't have to scurry around trying to find assistance to accomplish the task.

*Mr. M:*   That sounds like a reasonable idea. How do the rest of you feel about this? Do you see any other problem areas that we need to examine at this point? I trust that if there are any, you will bring them up at this point. Or is there anything specifically that we could reword or redesign that would make this new program better for us?

Note the difference between the first meeting and the second; a number of factors stand out. The whole approach of the manager in the second case is one of seeking out and requesting ideas from various members of the team. Team members participate; they feel more involved and committed and feel that their ideas have been heard. As a result, the overall quality of the plan is improved substantially. The facilitative skills demonstrated here include the following:

1.   Asking open-ended questions.
2.   Encouraging cross-discussion between members of the group.

3.  Listening actively.
4.  Playing back what one hears another person saying.
5.  Openly accepting the ideas of others.
6.  Recognizing how others feel about a proposal.

### Importance of Facilitation Skills

A directive approach tends to shut off the ideas of members. People hold back, differences are not aired, the problem-solving process is ignored, and, in general, decisions are the sole property of the manager. The net effect is that a plan will not succeed as well as it could have if there had been full cooperation and participation by all members of the team. On the other hand, a facilitative approach yields a number of positive results, including generating new ideas, identifying hidden problems, capitalizing on the synergy of the group, and building on the ideas of others. This approach reduces negative feelings between people and enhances cooperation; it increases trust within the group itself and creates an open atmosphere in which people are willing to share and exchange ideas; and it promotes professional development and growth because people are encouraged to improve. Facilitation skills lead to better problem solving and more correct decisions, ultimately resulting in higher productivity and increased quality. These skills include the following:

*Listening.* A successful manager is one who can listen and hear what other members of the team are saying. Active listening is important to successful team building.

*Asking Questions.* Managers need to know how to ask questions that sound like questions rather than veiled attempts at manipulation. Managers should ask questions that are open-ended and allow room for the individual to answer honestly, without fear that the answer is not the "right" one that the manager is seeking.

*Sharing Ideas and Feelings.* An effective team manager shares ideas and feelings and encourages others to do the same.

*Group Problem Solving.* Although managers usually know how to solve technical problems, they often have difficulty applying their problem-solving skills to organizational and personnel problems. Therefore, a manager must learn to use the standard problem-solving steps in a group setting. These steps are defining the problem, considering alternative ways of solving the problem, weighing the pros and cons of each alternative and selecting the best one, implementing an action plan, and evaluating the results.

*Conflict Resolution.* Effective team managers know how to resolve the conflict that will inevitably arise within their teams. Conflict should not be suppressed but should be examined and dealt with constructively.

*Participatory Style.* A participatory style of management must be used in a team-building effort. The very purpose of team building is to develop the involvement of all members. This cannot be done by using an authoritarian approach to managing.

*Acceptance.* Acceptance is a willingness to hear what others have to say, without ridiculing or putting down the people or their ideas. A manager should give people a fair chance to express their ideas and, if they are not feasible, carefully explain the reasons why they will not work.

*Empathy.* Managers and team members must learn how to be empathic toward other members of the team, to understand how another person feels, and to express this understanding to the other person.

*Group Leadership Skills.* All team members, not just managers, should develop group leadership skills. These skills include both tasks and maintenance: keeping the discussion on target and managing the way people interact with each other (managing the process). Keeping the discussion on target is done by initiating discussion and raising questions, mining all the hidden information from within the group, sharing all information with the rest of the team, stopping from time to time to make sure that all members know exactly what has gone on and what has been said, summarizing information so that all members can see what progress has been made, and assessing how members feel about their contributions and their readiness to continue toward the solution. Managing the process requires looking at both sides of issues and reducing the amount of tension between people with very different points of view; when people are reluctant to reveal what they have on their minds, helping them to speak up; making positive statements about members' contributions; finding ways to take the best of different points of view to arrive at a compromise solution; and looking at the net effect of suggested solutions and approaches to see whether they will actually work in the real world.

## Learning Facilitation Skills

A vice-president at a large chemical company was very skillful at developing potential among members of his staff and encouraging them to solve their own problems. When someone brought a problem to a staff meeting, he would ask the person to describe it to him and then he would respond with something like "That's interesting. Have you considered exploring this avenue?" From this he would lead to "What do you think some of the possible solutions are?" and then "Which of the possible options tends to be the best option?" He never directly told people what he expected of them during the course of the problem-solving process; instead, by using his facilitative skills, he guided them to the point where they solved their own problems. When asked where he learned his facilitation skills, he answered that he had observed them in a manager he had worked for in the past and realized that this approach was the most effective way to get results out of a team. He had also worked for a very aggressive, directive manager who got results, but at the expense of his staff. So he decided to start observing the behaviors of successful managers, to read books on the subject, to discuss the aspects of managing with other managers, and to attend a variety of seminars. He then started practicing what he had learned in his everyday managing. He had a strong and compelling drive to improve the way in which he was working with those who reported to him and over time was able to change to a facilitative approach. Once he had moved from his old approach to the facilitative approach, he could sense that his career was taking off. He ended up as a president of the chemical company.

To develop a clear picture of the differences between a directive manager and a facilitative manager, it is helpful to observe successful managers, those who get the best results over the long run. One should not, however, fall into the trap of thinking that the most successful manager is one who is able to coerce people into doing things in the short term, when in fact such policies will fail in the long run. There is an abundance of reading material, training programs, seminars, and workshops that can be used as aids in developing facilitative skills (see the Appendix for a representative list). Most important, the process of becoming a more facilitative team manager must be practiced on a day-to-day basis. It is usually best to start out working on a single skill, to learn that skill well, and then begin developing the other skills one at a time.

It can be useful to complete the self-assessment of team and interpersonal skills that is presented in Exhibit 8. This will help direct efforts at self-improvement and can also be used by team members to assess how the team is handling the leadership functions. An open discussion within the team of the points listed in this assessment is usually very productive.

## Exhibit 8. Inventory of Team and Interpersonal Managing Skills.

| | To What Extent Do You Need to Improve? | | |
|---|---|---|---|
| | *Very Little* | *Somewhat* | *Very Large* |
| *Relationships with Peers and Supervisors* | | | |
| 1. Competing with my peers | _____ | _____ | _____ |
| 2. Being open with my seniors | _____ | _____ | _____ |
| 3. Feeling inferior to colleagues | _____ | _____ | _____ |
| 4. Standing up for myself | _____ | _____ | _____ |
| 5. Building open relationships | _____ | _____ | _____ |
| 6. Following policy guidelines | _____ | _____ | _____ |
| 7. Questioning policy guidelines | _____ | _____ | _____ |
| *Team Dynamics* | | | |
| 8. Knowing other team members as individuals | _____ | _____ | _____ |
| 9. Meeting sufficiently often | _____ | _____ | _____ |
| 10. Supporting open expression of views | _____ | _____ | _____ |
| 11. Setting high standards | _____ | _____ | _____ |
| 12. Punishing behavior that deviates from the team norm | _____ | _____ | _____ |
| 13. Clarifying aims and objectives | _____ | _____ | _____ |
| 14. Giving information and views | _____ | _____ | _____ |
| 15. Using status to influence decisions of the team | _____ | _____ | _____ |
| 16. Delegating to reduce workload | _____ | _____ | _____ |
| *Relationships with Team Members* | | | |
| 17. Helping others identify problems | _____ | _____ | _____ |
| 18. Practicing counseling skills | _____ | _____ | _____ |
| 19. Being distant with some people | _____ | _____ | _____ |
| 20. Intervening when things go wrong | _____ | _____ | _____ |
| 21. Being strong when reprimanding | _____ | _____ | _____ |

**Exhibit 8. Inventory of Team and Interpersonal Managing Skills, Cont'd.**

| | | | | |
|---|---|---|---|---|
| 22. | Giving energy to others | _____ | _____ | _____ |
| 23. | Clarifying individual objectives | _____ | _____ | _____ |
| 24. | Supporting others in difficulties | _____ | _____ | _____ |
| 25. | Bringing problems out | _____ | _____ | _____ |
| 26. | Supporting risk taking | _____ | _____ | _____ |
| 27. | Being open in assessment of others | _____ | _____ | _____ |

*Relationships with Employees*

| | | | | |
|---|---|---|---|---|
| 28. | Being known as a person by employees | _____ | _____ | _____ |
| 29. | Being available to employees | _____ | _____ | _____ |
| 30. | Knowing how people feel | _____ | _____ | _____ |
| 31. | Acting to resolve conflicts | _____ | _____ | _____ |
| 32. | Emphasizing communication | _____ | _____ | _____ |
| 33. | Passing on information quickly | _____ | _____ | _____ |
| 34. | Emphasizing personal status | _____ | _____ | _____ |
| 35. | Bypassing management structure when communicating | _____ | _____ | _____ |

*Working in Groups*

| | | | | |
|---|---|---|---|---|
| 36. | Using a systematic approach | _____ | _____ | _____ |
| 37. | Developing others' skills | _____ | _____ | _____ |
| 38. | Being prompt | _____ | _____ | _____ |
| 39. | Using time effectively | _____ | _____ | _____ |
| 40. | Listening actively | _____ | _____ | _____ |
| 41. | Openly expressing views | _____ | _____ | _____ |
| 42. | Dominating others | _____ | _____ | _____ |
| 43. | Maintaining good group climate | _____ | _____ | _____ |
| 44. | Dealing constructively with disruptive behavior | _____ | _____ | _____ |
| 45. | Building informal contacts | _____ | _____ | _____ |

**Exhibit 8. Inventory of Team and Interpersonal Managing Skills, Cont'd.**

| | | | |
|---|---|---|---|
| 46. | Disparaging other groups | ___ ___ ___ |
| 47. | Sharing objectives with other groups | ___ ___ ___ |
| 48. | Identifying mutual communication needs | ___ ___ ___ |
| 49. | Arranging intergroup social events | ___ ___ ___ |
| 50. | Acting to resolve conflicts | ___ ___ ___ |

*Helping Others Improve*

| | | |
|---|---|---|
| 51. | Making time for counseling | ___ ___ ___ |
| 52. | Identifying the group's training needs | ___ ___ ___ |
| 53. | Setting coaching assignments | ___ ___ ___ |
| 54. | Allocating time and money for training | ___ ___ ___ |
| 55. | Giving feedback to others | ___ ___ ___ |
| 56. | Sharing parts of job for others' development | ___ ___ ___ |

*Self-Development*

| | | |
|---|---|---|
| 57. | Setting aside time to think | ___ ___ ___ |
| 58. | Visiting other organizations | ___ ___ ___ |
| 59. | Discussing principles and values | ___ ___ ___ |
| 60. | Taking on new challenges | ___ ___ ___ |
| 61. | Attending training events | ___ ___ ___ |
| 62. | Knowing when and how to use specialist resources | ___ ___ ___ |

# ✤ 10 ✤

# Building a
# Productive Team:
# Case Example

This chapter provides a comprehensive example that combines all of the elements of teamwork discussed in Chapter One. The company being examined is a multiproduct auto parts supply firm headquartered in a midwestern city. It has five plants with approximately 2,500 employees and a salary-exempt group of roughly 250 managers and supervisors. The company was originally part of a much larger corporation that was dismantled and its components sold. It had been through three different owners during a period of five years; the newest owners had acquired the company a year and a half earlier through a leveraged buyout (a large loan against assets), and the company was now striving to acquire related smaller companies to expand business. The company's top executive group, the focus of this case example, consisted of the CEO, two executive vice-presidents, the controller, the treasurer, and the vice-presidents for administration and employee relations. This group had been working together for several years; the only relative newcomer on the team was the treasurer, who had been appointed by the newest owners.

## Symptoms

The executive group had been experiencing considerable frustration as a result of the change of ownership and was also troubled by a major strike against the company that was in progress. Discussions between members of the organization, including two executives, and the consultant revealed an excessive amount of backbiting among and complaining about various members of the management team, and the one newcomer, the treasurer, was viewed as a "spy of the owners." There were general complaints about the length of time it took to make decisions. There was evidence that members of the team had broken into opposing factions, with the CEO and the two executive vice-presidents on one side and the remaining members of the team on the other. The members of the first faction were the primary decision makers who held the base of power; the members of the second faction felt subordinate and somewhat powerless. Several of the key executives reported that they were experiencing a significant amount of stress. This was particularly evident in two members of the group who were described as "tight as a wire." In many cases, these two were blowing up at each other, as well as at other members of the staff. They were showing physical signs of stress and openly admitted that things were getting to them.

At a meeting with the entire management group to talk out some of these problems, it became evident that the two executive vice-presidents were the primary sources of trouble for this team, as they dominated the discussions, were openly combative with other members of the team, and were frequently short-tempered. One member of the team, the vice-president for administration, assumed the role of an extremely sarcastic and caustic devil's advocate. There were observable signs that at least four members of the group—the two executive vice-presidents, the controller, and the vice-president for employee relations—were experiencing significant stress.

This team wasted many hours in lengthy and overly detailed discussions of trivial problems. During the annual compensation-adjustments review, the two executive vice-presidents entered into a long-winded discussion concerning the reasons that raises were being given to certain people while they also campaigned for raises for other people. This is not usually a topic that is dealt with in such depth at this level of an organization. These differences led to raised voices, long debates, and often a general exchange of put-downs and insults. There was also considerable friction surrounding decisions of greater import—the introduction of new programs or changes in existing programs.

The symptoms present in this organization point to a variety of possible breakdowns in the way the team was functioning: excessive concentration of interpersonal dynamics; a lack of clarity about the decision-making and problem-solving processes; an absence of goal identification; and problems in role clarification and communication. Table 2 describes and summarizes the symptoms and presents possible theoretical explanations.

## Collecting Data to Highlight Problems

The group decided to bring in outside consultants to assist in collecting additional information that could specifically identify the existing problems. Through discussions with the consultant, it was decided that an interview and questionnaire process should be used. The structure of the interview was geared to collect information about the management team's concerns about how the organization was being handled. The questionnaire was designed to uncover information about the performance of the team, task accomplishment, and the way in which members were working together. Finally, the Stress Processing Report, an evaluative instrument developed by Human Synergetics, was used to measure the team members' levels of stress. The interview revealed the following concerns about how the company was being managed (the numbers in parentheses indicate how many times each concern was mentioned):

Financial stability (5)
Always on a crisis basis (4)
Ownership changes (4)
Top management gets into too much detail (4)
Compensation system for top group (3)
Feelings of not being involved in overall management (3)
Too much attention paid to two top officers (2)
Too many end runs to the CEO (2)

Union situation (1)
No sense of urgency to solve problem (1)

### Table 2. Symptoms of Team Problems.

| Symptoms | Description | Explanation |
|---|---|---|
| Backbiting and complaining | Members of group openly complaining about and finding fault with each other | Lack of clarity about standards, loss of control over group members |
| Presence of "spy of owner" | Suspicion and distrust of new member of group | Difficulty of breaking into an established group |
| Two coalitions | Two groups, senior officers and junior officers, with junior group having very little influence or power | Lack of group cohesiveness |
| Personal stress | Stress showing up in three members, evident in "blowing up" and physical symptoms | People feeling threatened, thus becoming less efficient and more dissatisfied |
| Combative behavior | Yelling and directly combative behavior in the name of playing the devil's advocate | Conflict expressed through use of threats, attacks, and so on |
| Infinite details | Infinite detail and checking on all aspects of minor or major decisions | |
| Amount of time to make decisions | Minor decisions reaching top of organization and taking excessive time | Lack of trust directly related to group problem solving |
| Shifting and changing decisions | Decisions frequently changed shortly after being made | |

The information from the interviews was summarized and organized into a list of each executive's positive qualities and the specific behaviors of each that were causing problems for other members of the team. Responses included comments such as the following:

"He doesn't 'kick ass' when he should. He tries to be
   too nice of a guy."
"I don't trust him. I think he is the owners' spy."
"He gets too rigid at times, and he's unwilling to change."
"He doesn't listen to our needs, and he fails to under-
   stand what we are trying to accomplish."
"He has his hands in everything, controls all things, and
   doesn't delegate any responsibility."
"He fritters away too much time getting into the fine print
   of everything. He should be delegating more."
"He has no long-range plans. He needs to develop a
   strategy for what he is doing."

The purpose of providing this information was to enable each
member to make adjustments in personal and task behaviors
that would enhance the performance of the team.

The questionnaire responses revealed several areas that
received less than acceptable ratings: planning and organizing,
problem definition and solutions, and commitment to process.
The questionnaire is presented in Exhibit 9.

The information on stress outlined in Table 3 (measured
with the Stress Processing Report) revealed a significant amount
of stress within the management team. Thirty-two percent of
the responses indicated that stress was felt in relationships with
other people, and 43 percent indicated stress concerning the way
work was conducted. The stress instrument also measured the
extent of team members' satisfaction with such factors as personal life, work life, meaningfulness of life, financial situation,
and health. In general, the results were fairly positive. A summary of the individual data revealed that three members of the
group were experiencing excessive levels of stress. Further investigation determined that their stress was caused principally
by insufficient time allotted for accomplishing required tasks;
a self-imposed "read the clock" orientation; a sense of inability
to control events; activities being imposed on the members by
others; and lack of cooperation between members. Clearly, the
situation faced by this management group reflected a work environment that was a breeding ground for high levels of stress.

## Exhibit 9. Management Team Effectiveness.

*Rating Scale* (Circle composite or overall team rating)

| 1 | 2 | 3 | 4 | 5 |
|---|---|---|---|---|
| Team does not meet task requirements | Team meets some task requirements | Team meets the major task requirements | Team meets all task requirements | Team consistently exceeds expectations |

### Task

1. *Planning and Organizing*

   How well do the planning and organizing of this team prepare it to accomplish its tasks?

   ```
            x
            x  x  x
            x  x  x
     1   2   3   4   5
   ```

   Comments:

2. *Problem Definition and Solution*

   How well does this team define and solve the problems it faces?

   ```
         x
         x
         x  x
         x  x           x
     1   2   3   4   5
   ```

   Comments:

3. *Control*

   How effective are the controls that this team establishes to ensure that results are achieved as planned?

   ```
         x   x
         x   x
         x   x   x
     1   2   3   4   5
   ```

   Comments:

4. *Goals and Objectives*

   How well does this team meet the goals and objectives it establishes?

   ```
              x
          x   x   x
          x   x   x
     1   2   3   4   5
   ```

   Comments:

5. *Follow-Up*

   How well does this team follow up or take corrective action when needed?

   ```
              x
              x
          x   x           x
     1   2   3   4   5
   ```

   Comments:

Exhibit 9. Management Team Effectiveness, Cont'd.

## Process

1 = Minimal teamwork conditions   5 = Ideal teamwork conditions

1. *Listening*

Members don't really listen to each other, interrupt.

```
                x
          x     x     x
          x     x     x
     1    2     3     4     5
```

All members really listen, try hard to understand and are understood.

Comments:

2. *Communications*

Guarded, cautious

```
                      x
                      x
                      x     x
                x     x     x
     1    2     3     4     5
```

Open, authentic

Comments:

3. *Attitudes Toward Differences Within Group*

Members avoid arguments, smooth over differences, avoid conflicts.

```
                x
                x
                x     x
          x     x     x
     1    2     3     4     5
```

Members search for, respect, and accept differences and work them through openly as a team.

Comments:

4. *Involvement and Participation*

Discussion is dominated by a few members.

```
                x
          x     x
          x     x     x     x
     1    2     3     4     5
```

All members are involved, free to participate in the way they want.

Comments:

5. *Commitment*

Members have little commitment to team effort.

```
          x
          x
          x     x
          x     x     x     x
     1    2     3     4     5
```

All members have high commitment to the team's effort. All work hard to get a good team solution and are committed to team's decisions.

Comments:

**Exhibit 9. Management Team Effectiveness, Cont'd.**

6. *Mutual Support*

|  |  |  |  |  |  |
|---|---|---|---|---|---|
|  |  | x | x |  |  |
|  | x | x | x | x | x |
| 1 | 2 | 3 | 4 | 5 |  |

Members are indifferent to needs or concerns of others.

Comments:

Members get help from others on the team and give help, have genuine concern for each other.

7. *Flexibility*

|  |  |  |  |  |  |
|---|---|---|---|---|---|
|  |  |  | x |  |  |
|  |  |  | x |  |  |
|  |  |  | x |  |  |
|  |  | x | x |  |  |
| 1 | 2 | 3 | 4 | 5 |  |

Group is locked in on established rules. Members find it hard to change procedures.

Comments:

Members readily change procedures to meet situation.

**Table 3. Stress Processing Report.**

Percentage of High-Stress Areas Related to:

|  |  |  | *Percentage* |
|---|---|---|---|
| Self | 9 out of 42 | = | 21% |
| Others | 9 out of 28 | = | 32% |
| Process | 15 out of 35 | = | 43% |
| Goals | 5 out of 28 | = | 18% |

Specific Areas of Stress for the Group:

| Control | 4 out of 7 |
|---|---|
| Intimacy | 4 out of 7 |
| Cooperation | 4 out of 7 |
| Time orientation | 3 out of 7 |
| Time use | 3 out of 7 |
| Future | 3 out of 7 |

## Description of the Problem

To spur on this management group to collectively work on solving their problems and increase their ability to function as an effective team, the data that had been collected had to be presented in a format that succinctly highlighted the key issues and sparked the team into action. The presentation of information had to be realistic, meaningful, and accurate if team members were to be willing to accept and act on it. Because some of the information was highly sensitive, it was presented to team members individually rather than revealed in front of the team as a whole. This was particularly true of the stress data. Generalized information was presented to the whole team, while specific individual data were discussed in one-on-one counseling sessions. If team members decided to share their individual data with the rest of the team, they were free to do so. The presentation and feedback of the data proceeded from generalized to specific information.

During a team session, an informal discussion was conducted to explain how to use the information and, specifically, how to develop an understanding of its significance. The information was presented in the following order: general information on the way the company was being managed; information on the management of team effectiveness; and a summary of the individual data (a generalized report about the level of stress within the organization). The team then focused on the problem areas that they felt were most critical to improving the way the team was functioning: inadequate planning on the part of the management team; inefficient team problem solving; weak and ineffective control; organizational and team functions; a generally low level of commitment to team effectiveness; and the high levels of stress experienced by various members of the team.

Although the members of the team agreed that these were the primary areas of concern, and that it was fairly evident how these problems were developing within the team, there was disagreement as to which areas should be regarded as most important. After a lengthy discussion, the team decided to consider planning, problem solving, and control as a single problem area; they regarded this problem area as a weakness in the leadership of the team, due primarily to the performance of the CEO, whose management style was rather loose and of the laissez-faire variety. The team felt that a more aggressive and hard-hitting leadership style was needed, at least until the team and the company got back on their feet. Their conclusions can be summarized as follows:

*Planning, problem solving, and control:* Inadequate and poorly coordinated planning, problem solving, and control of management activities largely resulted from the laid-back style of the CEO, who did not set clear and high expectations for the management team. Furthermore, he encouraged dominance by two members of the team over other team members.

*Commitment:* Commitment grows out of mutual problem solving. In the case of this management team, with the exception of two members, the way the group functioned encouraged individual differences and discouraged cooperation and mutual support.

*Stress:* Stress grew out of four factors: dissension in the management team, uncertainty caused by reorganization (new ownership), the major strike, and uncertainty about market conditions.

The team elected to drop the question of team commitment, assuming that if a stronger leadership style were adopted, a stronger commitment would follow. They also decided that each team member should go through individual counseling sessions to personally diagnose and subsequently reduce their levels of stress. Now that the team had identified two critical areas, the next step was to develop action plans aimed at handling these problems on a day-to-day basis.

## Action Planning

The members of the management team arranged individual meetings with an outside consultant to discuss their stress data. The three members with the highest stress levels expressed relief that their situation had been recognized, and they began steps to reduce their stress. Following these sessions, a series of three off-site meetings focused on more effective planning, problem solving, and controlling.

At the first meeting, the team decided to ask the CEO to take a stronger position in developing a clear and accepted process for forecasting and setting organizational goals (for the current year and the next five years). They also decided to work collectively, under the guidance of an expert strategic planning consultant, to formulate plans and methods of implementation. They assigned individual responsibilities for seeking out a consultant, setting up time frames, and carrying out other tasks that would get the ball rolling.

The second meeting of the series was devoted to discussing the problem-solving and decision-making processes, particularly the major problem that had been identified: that two members of the group were dominating the decision-making and problem-solving processes and other members were taking a backseat to them. The team agreed to develop a format that included more active involvement of secondary members and that provided for activities to be monitored to ensure that the two aggressive members did not continue their domination. They also agreed to study the pertinent literature on problem solving and decision making and, if necessary, to bring in a consultant to help develop their skills in these areas.

The third meeting focused on the control aspect of the way the team was being managed. After a lengthy discussion, the team decided that it would be inappropriate to set up control procedures and mechanisms until the planning and goal-setting processes had been established. The logic behind this decision was that a process must be understood before it can be governed. The rest of the meeting was devoted to a discussion of the CEO's leadership style. Over the course of the three meetings, he had been trying to take a more aggressive and dominant role. The team members felt that he was succeeding in this and that he should be encouraged to continue. There was some concern, however, that he might continue to use this style even after the team began to manage itself more efficiently and that the team should identify the point at which he should begin to back off.

At the end of the meeting, the team members agreed to continue to seek ways to help each other grow and improve and to establish methods for countering unproductive behaviors. By this time, members of the team had reviewed their own individual data, accepted the results, and agreed to make changes. They decided to hold a special meeting to discuss the impact of individual styles on members of the team and to analyze those behaviors that had a negative impact on the team. They also decided to conclude each future meeting with a discussion of any interpersonal issues that had cropped up during that meeting. The team's final action plans are presented in Table 4.

**Table 4. Action Plans.**

| Problem Area | Date | Responsibility | Actions |
|---|---|---|---|
| Stress | Individually set | Individual | Meet with consultant to discuss results of stress questionnaire |
| Leadership | ASAP | CEO | Examine his leadership style and start to take a stronger role in setting expectations for the management group |
| Planning | August 20 | Specific members of team | Design, with assistance from outside consultant, a strategic planning process accepted by all team members |
| Problem solving | September 15 | Appointed member of group | Develop a process for more active involvement of all team members; review literature on best ways to problem solve as a group |
| Interpersonal relationships | December 1 | Members of group | Share personal data on stress and receive feedback from other members of the group |

## Implementation and Evaluation

The members of the management team implemented their plans and even went beyond the original intentions of their efforts to come up with a statement of "unity of purpose." This statement was developed according to the steps shown in Figure 4. Development of such a statement suggests that the team-building exercise that this team was engaged in had been successful. The effect of this effort was felt throughout the company.

The team developed a model of how they wanted to manage overall organizational improvement and effectiveness, and this model is shown in Figure 5. The net result of this effort

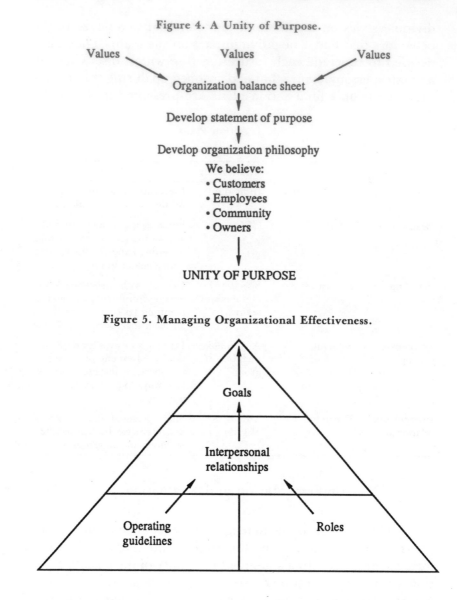

Figure 4. A Unity of Purpose.

Values ———→  Values  ←——— Values
                 ↓
      Organization balance sheet
                 ↓
      Develop statement of purpose
                 ↓
      Develop organization philosophy
            We believe:
            • Customers
            • Employees
            • Community
            • Owners
                 ↓
         UNITY OF PURPOSE

Figure 5. Managing Organizational Effectiveness.

Goals

Interpersonal
relationships

Operating
guidelines

Roles

was a substantial improvement in the way in which business was conducted as a whole. This progress was noted not only by people within the organization but also by former owners and by officials of the local government. Although it was evident that the team's efforts had begun to reduce stress and that its direction had become more clearly focused, the team decided to conduct a reevaluation that utilized an assessment questionnaire. The results indicated significant improvement in all pertinent areas. To ensure that they did not lapse into any previous bad habits or patterns, the team members decided to continue with regular assessment. Through sustained and systematic efforts, this team was able to dramatically improve its effectiveness. There are three keys to success in such an endeavor: a careful and complete analysis of the problem, accurately laid plans for correction, and committed follow-through and review.

# ❧ 11 ❧

# Starting New Teams

New teams are formed nearly every day in most organizations; teams come in the form of task forces, committees, project staffs, new departments, study groups, and so forth. Careful planning in the development of a new team can make the difference between a productive and an unproductive team. Unfortunately, many managers leave to chance the process of forming and building new teams or simply rely on the unstructured process of human interaction. Establishing a positive and productive team environment is one of the most important functions a manager can perform.

A significant body of knowledge concerning how people function in groups, much of it based on common sense, has been accumulated over the years. Since a considerable portion of this knowledge has been derived from the direct observation of groups in action, it is sometimes difficult for managers to appreciate the value of in-depth examination of a familiar situation. An accurate comprehension of how people function within the group setting will serve as a reliable guide in the effort to improve teamwork effectiveness. Many managers have developed the unfortunate habit of flying by the seat of their pants, ignoring many of the subtleties of team management. When a teamwork problem arises, it is often tempting to jump to conclusions that point at quick-fix solutions. But building on what is already known will establish a point to move forward from and prevent wasting effort on strategies that have already been proved fruitless.

### Learning from Others' Experience

The failure to use available knowledge can lead to team problems, as the following illustration painfully points out. A

112

large hospital in a southern city was managed by a sister of one
of the large Catholic orders. She had just established her top
team and was moving rapidly to build team spirit. She had
discovered that some members of her staff were not working
together, so she requested help from a consultant to solve the
problem with her staff before it got worse. The consultant conducted individual interviews, during which he asked people to
discuss the strengths and weaknesses of each member of the
management team, and administered a questionnaire that measured personality characteristics. The interviews revealed a
strong sense of loyalty to the hospital and its basic growth plans
but poor interpersonal relationships between two or three team
members, with distrust and a failure to pull together. A telling
discovery was that the administrator had used fear tactics to
coerce employees into meeting their objectives. Though she had
insisted on one-on-one communication, her idea of one-on-one
communication was to talk at (not listen to) the individual members of the team and to prevent them from speaking honestly
among themselves; she had clearly stated that she intended to
take action where necessary to correct improper performance
on the part of each member. She wanted complete control over
the lines of communication between the members of the management team.

   The consultant decided to use a form of team building
that had proved successful in similar situations: an open structure that would force members of the team to reveal their feelings about one another. In a meeting with the team, he asked
the team members to take turns discussing their survey results;
after each person spoke, the other members of the team would
provide input and clarification. The administrator was the second person to speak. As she began going over her data, she
became very defensive, finally asking members of the team to
give her more clarification. Response was almost nonexistent;
what little input was provided was on the positive side. When
the consultant asked for a third person to step forward, there
were no volunteers. The administrator kept pushing for someone
to "take responsibility for their own actions" in order to move
ahead with the team-building session; she finally ordered a particular team member to produce her data. This reluctant "volun-

teer" complied in a very guarded and hesitant manner, and no one but the administrator dared to respond. After this, no one would volunteer to speak, and the administrator was unable to force anyone to. The team-building process had sputtered to an end. The exasperated administrator decided to call off the whole process. The first attempt at team building had been smothered, and any future attempts were placed in serious jeopardy.

When a leader uses an autocratic or punitive style of management, people are going to be guarded and fearful, and there will be a low level of trust. In the above case, the administrator's prevailing punitive style was the major contributor to the breakdown of the team-building effort. Had the consultant, along with a more cooperative administrator, carefully thought through the specific problems and the known methods applicable to such problems, the design of the team-building strategy might have been quite different and more successful. The data collected in the interviews showed that there was conflict and failure to share objectives among members of the management team. This suggests that a conflict-resolution strategy, rather than an interpersonal-sharing strategy, would have been more appropriate and more productive.

The interview data in this case indicated that the members of the management team were loyal, that they focused on the goals achieved, and that they were willing to put forth the effort required to move the organization forward. Given the poor interpersonal relationships and the counterproductive administrative style, an initial team-building strategy that focused on goal setting might also have been successful. With this approach, a successful group goal setting effort might well have done much to dispel the group's mistrust and conflict and opened the administrator's eyes to both the negativity of her own style of leadership and her role in the group's previous failures.

This case illustrates three important components in the correct design of a team-building strategy for a new team: understanding what the preliminary data reveal about the members of the team; being familiar with a variety of available team-building strategies; and matching the appropriate strategy to the specific situation exposed by the preliminary data.

## Understanding How People Work Together

Whenever a manager is organizing a new team, it is important to step back and study how individual backgrounds interact to produce results. Team leaders need to learn how to adjust personal and group factors in order to encourage teamwork and achieve group goals. Berelson and Steiner (1964) offer useful guidelines for forming a new team, summarized below:

*Structure and Size of Team*
- The most desirable group size is approximately five members.
- The larger the percentage of new members in an existing group, the more resistance there will be to their assimilation.

*Physical Surroundings*
- Poor surroundings deter effectiveness.
- Groups tend to lay claim to fixed sites and familiar places.
- Face-to-face seating is most useful in problem solving.

*Goals*
- When there are no established goals or bases for measuring group results, a group tends to be unstable and unpredictable.
- A group is less likely to support or achieve goals that are imposed from the outside.
- The effectiveness of a group improves when personal goals are incorporated into the achievement of group goals.
- Active group participation in goal setting is more effective than goal setting on an exclusively individual basis.

*Tasks*
- Groups have to alternate sometimes conflicting roles, such as dealing directly with the task or attending to the emotional and social relationships within the group. Concentration on the first role leads to tension; concentration on the second reduces that tension.
- Group tasks include initiating and contributing, information seeking and giving, opinion seeking and giving, elaborating, coordinating, recording, orienting, evaluating, energizing, and procedural management.

*Group Norms*
- The more individuals share in and agree on group norms, the more they will like each other.
- Smaller groups strongly influence the behavior of their members by setting and enforcing norms.
- Members of a group are ranked according to how closely they conform to the group's norms; the more closely they conform, the higher they rank.
- The less clear a group is about its standards, the less control it exerts over its members.

*Leadership*
- Leadership (formal or informal) tends to be assigned to the person who most closely conforms to the standards set by the group and who displays the most knowledge and skill.
- When a group is already established, it is extremely difficult for a new leader to shift the group's activities or direction.
- The longer a particular person remains in the leadership position, the less open and free the communication tends to be, and the less efficient the solutions to new problems are.
- In the group setting, authoritarian leaders are less effective than democratic leaders.
- A leader must meet two simultaneous needs of the group: the need to initiate, guide, and contribute and the need to harmonize, help, and mutually share.
- The most effective group leaders are hard workers, have high task and ability orientation, and are liked by team members.
- Experienced, effective group leaders capitalize on interpersonal processes to maximize the performance of their groups.

*Individual Team Member Behavior*
- New members of a group usually feel inferior to the established members.
- An individual will not usually hold out against the weight of a group decision, even when the group is in error.
- The more threatened an individual feels, the more concerned with acceptance and the less efficient and satisfied he or she becomes.

- The more compatible the behaviors, skills, and status of group members are, the more that group procedures and norms are accepted.

*Reward and Punishment*
- A group rewards or punishes individual behaviors in relation to their acceptance by the group.

*Trust*
- Trust plays a significant role in group problem-solving effectiveness.
- Trust is built through behaviors that convey appropriate information, permit mutual influence, encourage self-control, and avoid abusing the vulnerability of others.

*Conflict*
- The least successful strategies for resolving conflict are those that involve threats, attacks, and forced compliance or compromise.
- The most successful strategies are those that work toward mutually beneficial outcomes, propose package deals, and establish systematic concessions.

*Change*
- The less change is imposed on a group, the higher the general level of group satisfaction is.
- The more cohesive a group is, the more individuals are attracted to the group.
- When change is desired, it is more effective to approach and influence the group as a whole than to approach and influence the individual members.

Although there are a variety of approaches to adjusting personal and group factors, the following four steps usually prove useful. First, conduct a thorough analysis of either the nature of the team that is to be established or the specific problems that are to be corrected within an existing team. Collect information about how individuals behave and their feelings about the team through both observation and interviews. Second, sort and arrange the collected information, with particular attention to inconsistencies or potential problems in the way the team is functioning; for example, lack of clarity about the team goal or serious differences between two people's ideas about how to get a job done. Third, consult the established knowledge base. Compare the nature of the group problem with what is known about the group and then focus on strategies that best fit the problem at hand. Finally, design the strategy that will be the most productive for solving the specific problems that have been identified.

When a team of five university professors was assigned the task of developing a new graduate program, the team leader analyzed the factors that were most likely to influence the way the team would function once they started to work together. He found that the group shared a common goal, which was to establish the graduate degree program; strong dominant leadership would be met with resistance, but sharing the leadership responsibility would be welcome; where roles were undefined as a result of special interests, there was a likelihood of conflict and tasks being avoided because of lack of interest; the rewards for completing the assigned task were a sense of achievement and an opportunity to teach at the graduate level.

Given these discoveries, the team leader called a meeting to discuss how the group could set itself up to accomplish its task. Members identified their personal goals, selected their roles and assignments, agreed on how they would conduct their meetings (dates, times, procedures, and so on), and, most important, agreed on how they would resolve potential problems. As a result of this early planning, the team successfully developed the new graduate degree program and became the core faculty.

## Forming New Teams

Because the life of most teams is quite short, managers are more likely to find themselves involved in setting up new teams than in trying to repair old ones. If a new team is to be forward-looking, its efforts and ideas should not be encumbered by practices and notions of past teams. The following suggestions will help ensure that a new team gets off to a good start.

## Selecting Team Members

Individual differences can occasionally cause problems in a team. If one member, for example, believes fervently in participation while another supports following the dictates of the leader, excessive time can be spent attempting to settle their differences. A manager who has the opportunity to select the members of a new team should consider a number of factors to ensure a positive chemistry among members once the team is in operation.

**Age.** Mixing people with extreme age differences can sometimes lead to problems that stem from the divergent sets of values often held by separate generations. Although there are times when a thirty-year age difference does not matter, it is best for a manager to know ahead of time whether the "old goats" and the "young pups" will get along.

**Individual Skills.** The tasks to be performed by the group dictate the types of skills that members possess. This often means that certain members have highly technical skills, and each member of a team must respect the expertise of the others.

**Attitudes.** It is not uncommon for people to be placed on teams that they do not initially wish to join. If a job is to be completed, it is essential that reluctant members develop a positive attitude.

**Team Skills.** People with teamwork experience can bring valuable assets to a team. If new team members are unfamiliar with teamwork skills, they should be trained in them as soon as possible.

## Steps in the Start-Up of a New Team

Unfortunately, teams are frequently allowed to simply drift into existence through a limp and lazy process that lacks careful management during the formative period. The following steps will enhance the likelihood that a team will get off on the right foot.

*Getting Acquainted.* All new teams need time for members to get to know each other: who they are, what their special skills are, what they have accomplished in the past, how they feel about being on the team, how committed they are to the project, and what their expectations are. The get-acquainted period is when trust and cohesiveness are built. Openness and the sharing of information lead people to feel more at home and more comfortable with others on the team.

*Clarifying Goals.* The next step is to clarify and define the team's goals: what should be the end result of the team's effort, what should be the benchmark goals along the way, and what subgoals should be assigned to individual team members. Ambiguity can act as a severe deterrent to meeting team objectives; every effort should be made to ensure that team members understand and agree with the team's goals.

*Team Management Philosophy.* It is extremely important that how the team will function be defined at the very beginning. Deciding how the team will be managed is usually based on considerations such as the task to be accomplished (Does it require innovation? Does it require routine accomplishments? Is the project under different time constraints?); the management style of the team leader (the manager should present and explain the style of managing that will be practiced); and the nature of the team members (the manager should seek to form a team that will function well under the desired style of management).

*Designing Operating Rules.* There are several operating rules that should be defined early in a team's life. Who is going to be the team leader? The manager usually takes this responsibility, but it can be shared and rotated among other team members. How will team members' conflict be handled? How will decisions be made? Will decision making be shared, or will all decisions be made by the team leader? Will consensus be used, or majority rule? Does the team have the authority to make decisions? All members of the team should be clear about their roles and the roles of other team members. To accomplish team goals, members must do their job and meet their individual goals. Whether the team goal is met is the ultimate measure, but how will progress be measured as the job moves ahead? Will it be known how well each team member is performing?

Meeting schedules and agendas of meetings can also be important to a team's success. The team should decide when and where the team will meet, how long the meetings should be, whether agendas will be used, whether minutes will be taken, and whether meetings will include discussions of ways to improve them. Ground rules should also be established to ensure that everyone's ideas and inputs are obtained and that ideas will be properly evaluated.

The time used to establish goals and guidelines is time well spent, since it should eliminate many mishaps, conflicts, wasted time, and gaps in getting the work done. Now the team is ready to move ahead with its tasks. Time should be set aside at all meetings to review the progress of both the team and individual team members. This monitoring has two purposes: to measure progress and to solve problems and remove bottlenecks as they occur. It also provides an opportunity to change operating rules that have not proved effective.

### Building a Productive Team Environment

The objective of team building is to establish a team culture that produces a high level of performance. There are several basic principles to remember when attempting to accomplish this goal:

- *Sharing information builds trust.* Being open and aboveboard with team members is the way trust is built. Trust means that individuals can depend on each other to do their jobs; it eliminates the need to guard against what others do and ensures that the best ideas come to the surface.
- *Shared problem solving produces the best answers.* If a problem is to be clearly understood and its best solution divined, everyone must be involved. Involvement will guarantee that all aspects of the problem are examined and that a complete array of possible solutions are considered.

- *How the team works together determines how effective it will be.* Do not deal just with the team's tasks and goals; talk about how the team works and develop ways to make it work better. Doing this can get the bugs out of the system and provide an opportunity for team members to vent their feelings and ideas.
- *The team should always be open and flexible to ideas and change.* We live in a dynamic world in which change seems to be the only constant. Being aware of change and willing to adjust to it renders the team more viable and better able to accomplish its goals.

# ✤ 12 ✤

# Training Managers
# in How to Build
# Productive Teams

A midlevel manager in a large energy company decided that he was going to find ways to improve the productivity of his management team, whose nine members performed a variety of technical functions. He had observed a number of dysfunctional qualities in his team, including a high level of conflict among members, misunderstanding about the team's goals, and a failure to utilize some of the members' competencies and skills. Having had no prior experience in team building or training in the field, the manager set out to educate himself about how to improve team productivity. He read several books and articles on the subject and talked with other members of his organization who had been through team-building experiences. Most of his sources suggested that team building could be conducted only with the aid of a facilitator. This was not what he had hoped he would find; he was determined to improve productivity on his own. He decided to use a model similar to the one discussed throughout this book: uncovering the team problems, defining them clearly, planning and implementing action steps to correct them, and evaluating the results to make certain that the goals are achieved. The manager gained the commitment of his team to the process and set about collecting the pertinent information. This information was assembled by a third party and presented to the team. The team then proceeded through the steps of problem definition, developing an action plan, and implementing that plan. The manager achieved the kind of change he was looking for, and the team members concluded that they had successfully improved teamwork and team productivity. The manager learned several things about team building through this process: (1) Team building is something that can be performed and managed by a team leader without the aid of outside consultation or facilitation. (2) It takes commitment on the part of all team members to solve problems and improve teamwork. (3) Managers must develop their own team management skills to perform the role of facilitator. (4) Team members have as much need to improve team productivity as does the team leader. This chapter provides ideas to help managers become qualified to direct their own team-building activities and decrease their dependence on outside facilitators.

There are several factors that need to be considered as assumptions when the issue of training managers to become self-directing in building their own teams is addressed:

There must be a high level of commitment on the part of the team itself; the team must see the value of increasing and improving the quality and quantity of its output; teams members must see the payoff not only in terms of the quality and quantity of their output but also in the satisfaction they feel toward the work that they perform; and teams need to recognize the value of improving team productivity from the point of view of creativity and innovation and how this view in turn will affect the performance of the team. If a team is not prepared to accept these assumptions prior to the team-building effort, the whole process will probably be futile and a waste of time.

Furthermore, for teamwork to improve through any type of training effort, the process must involve the entire team, not just selected members, and the team must be highly committed to the effort. Team members must recognize the need for improvement and be able to see the potential payoffs of the training effort. Another important point is that teams that go through team-building training need to have an environment that reinforces the learning that results from training activity. This is largely a function of the interest that the organization as a whole shows in effective teamwork and its overall philosophy of managing.

In order for team training to be effective, a manager must examine the backgrounds, personalities, and skills of the team members and any other factors that affect the way they work together. Training can then be designed around the areas where members of the team need the most assistance. A typical program requires all team members, regardless of their skill level, to go through the training process. Teamwork training sessions should be conducted with all team members present, because success is more likely when team members go through training as a group than when individual members attend team-training programs and then bring their newfound knowledge and experience back to the rest of the team.

## The Role of a Facilitator

Many training and development professionals believe that a team-development activity should involve a third party to serve as a facilitator to help move the team in the desired direction. This belief grew out of a long study of team-building activities, especially the early work done with sensitivity groups (T-groups) during the 1950s. T-groups were highly unstructured and required supervision to ensure that the team did not drift off into unproductive types of activities. In addition, early students of team building assumed that most managers lacked the skills and competencies required to manage teams effectively. Most theorists now believe, however, that managers can learn the necessary facilitation skills on their own and that these skills can become part of day-to-day management practices. Of course, the involvement of a third party is not always without merit; it is often recommended as an initial practice as long as the facilitator does not so dominate the process that the team becomes dependent on him or her. An outside team facilitator should be viewed as a trainer that helps the team learn how to manage its own activities.

## Design for Training Teams

An effective method for team training involves the following steps: (1) an idea, skill, or concept is presented in a lecture format; (2) it is then demonstrated through some behavioral format, such as role play; (3) members of the team practice using the idea, skill, or concept; and (4) they select a method for self-evaluation and feedback to measure their progress. If need be, this process can be repeated for more practice. Ultimately, the process is integrated into the daily practices of the team.

A popular type of training session is a two- or three-day off-site meeting where the team meets with a facilitator to examine problems and develop action plans. Another approach is to bring several teams together in a conference setting, combining general sessions where the training issues are presented in a seminar format and individual team sessions where each team practices the development of the new skills they have learned with the help of a team facilitator. A typical schedule for such a conference approach might be as follows:

*Day One*
1.  Introduction and overview.
2.  Observation of team in action: evaluating team performance.
3.  Discussion of team skills: listening, seeking information, giving information.
4.  Feedback on team performance (2 above).
5.  Observation of team in action: analysis of factors affecting teamwork and identification of key opportunities for improvement.

*Day Two*
6.  Discussion of personality as a factor in teamwork; feedback on personality data collected through instruments such as Myers-Briggs, Birkman, Acumen.
7.  Discussion of team skills: building an idea; testing understanding; proposing.
8.  Feedback on team performance (5 above).
9.  Observation of team in action: definition of team problems revealed by data about how the team functions.

*Day Three*
10. Continued discussion of personality as a factor in teamwork.
11. Discussion of team skills: bringing people in, supporting, summarizing.

12.   Feedback on team performance (9 above).
13.   Observation of team in action: developing alternative solutions to problems and checking implications.
*Day Four*
14.   Discussion of personality as a factor in teamwork, integrating previous discussions.
15.   Feedback on team performance (13 above).
16.   Discussion of design of action plans and evaluation process; testing implementation problems and commitment level.

A multiteam approach can be used; the collective training can promote mutual understanding, a shared vocabulary, and a common direction, thereby enhancing and reinforcing the culture when teams return to their work environment. This approach has been thoroughly tested in several large corporations and has proved to be highly effective in enabling teams to integrate their learning in their day-to-day activities. An organization that uses this method expresses a deep commitment to helping teams improve.

## Team Training Evaluation

Even the largest investment in training can be useless if the ongoing results of the training are not examined and evaluated. It is essential that any team-building training activity include a follow-up evaluation process to determine how well teams have improved their effectiveness and what result this has on their productivity. This can be done by conducting a survey of the factors affecting the way the team is working, examining output measures (amount and quality of work produced by the team), or testing team members' perceptions of team productivity and satisfaction. The method that most frequently appeals to management is the measurement of output. Whatever the evaluation process, it should be built in to the initial design of the training and made a part of the contract to which teams agree.

# ❧ 13 ❧

# Creating a
# Productive Team Culture

The most important task a team leader can perform is to create and manage a productive culture. A vital culture lets members know what is expected of them in various situations, which decreases the need for formal information and control systems and promotes the development of self-directed teams. When people have the opportunity to manage their own activities within the context of a broader culture, they have a strong sense of obligation to themselves, to their team, and to the entire organization. The common trait of successful leaders is their ability to develop such a positive team environment. A manager needs both vision and skill to articulate and bring to life a positive team culture. A team leader cannot play a passive role in developing and strengthening the culture.

## Definition of Organizational Culture

Culture is a social energy that can move people to act. Culture is to an organization what personality is to an individual: a hidden yet unifying theme that provides meaning, direction, and mobilization for the organization (Ott, 1989). Organizational culture includes the following elements:

1.  Observed behavior regularities—things that people do consistently.
2.  Norms that evolve out of the work group, such as the concept of a fair day's work for a fair day's pay.

128

3.   Dominant values embraced by the group, such as hard work, quality, or leadership.
4.   A philosophy of participation and involvement that guides the organization to accomplish its goals.
5.   A set of rules regarding how to get along within the team itself.
6.   A climate in which people desire to be members and to participate in the activities of the team.

For the manager, the most important aspects of organizational culture are that it is socially acquired and mutually shared and that it embodies the specific and general ways in which the team functions. Managers and team members do have the ability to shape cultures. As with the shaping of any culture, facts, truths, realities, beliefs, values, and practices are basically determined by members of the group. Many times, these cultural characteristics are not explicitly or consciously developed. Members often come to agree on things slowly and without much thought. It is the role and responsibility of a team leader to guide the positive direction of the culture that he or she desires for the team.

## The Evolution of Team Culture

Schein (1985) has outlined the stages in the evolution of group culture, as presented in Table 5. During the formation stage, the leader plays an important role in helping team members to understand the basic culture that they are entering. During the group building stage, team members begin to focus on the cultural beliefs and values of their team. This is where the team truly starts to become a team. The third stage begins when team members start to work together, when missions and tasks emerge and interdependencies become clear. Finally, when maturity is achieved, the group begins to function efficiently and clearly, with all members of the team involved.

Changes in team membership affect the culture of the team. When new members join a team, it is sometimes difficult to find time for the team to again progress through the four stages, and teams often disband before group maturity can be

Table 5. Stages of Group Evolution.

| Stage | Dominant Assumption | Socioemotional Focus |
|---|---|---|
| 1. Group formation | Dependence: "The leader knows what we should do." | Self-orientation; focus on issues of (1) inclusion, (2) power and influence, (3) acceptance and intimacy, (4) identity and role |
| 2. Group building | Fusion: "We are a great group; we all like each other." | Group as idealized object; focus on harmony, conformity, and search for intimacy; member differences not valued |
| 3. Group work | Work: "We can perform effectively because we all like each other." | Group mission and tasks; focus on accomplishment, teamwork, and maintaining the group in good working order; member differences valued |
| 4. Group maturity | Maturity: "We know who we are, what we want, and how to get it. We have been successful, so we must be right." | Group survival and comfort; focus on preserving the group and its culture; creativity and member differences seen as threat |

established. It is important for a manager to recognize at which stage a reformed team is functioning and to move ahead as rapidly as is prudent to get the team up and running. There is no standard timetable for progressing through the four stages; it can take several hours or several months. The importance and urgency of a team's objectives and the amount of time available for a team to work together are the factors that determine the timetable.

The most important objective for a team leader is to progress as rapidly as possible to the team maturity level and then maintain that level for as long as possible. Numerous forces are constantly bombarding teams and disrupting their culture. Many of these forces come from outside the control of the team; a team needs to be able to recognize these forces, reexamine the functions of the team in light of their effects on the team culture, and take corrective measures.

Managers need to consider several key elements of the internal structure of a culture when they attempt to sustain a positive environment (Ott, 1989). The first of these is the selection of team members. How new team members fit into the structure of the existing team is influenced by their personal values, beliefs, and perceptions about the way a team functions. When new members enter the team setting, a socialization process takes place: the new members learn the values, beliefs, and organizational rules associated with the team. A large part of the responsibility for this rests in the hands of the team leader. However, it is not uncommon for all team members to participate in the socialization process; team members can often help newcomers to learn the ground rules and norms for working in that team. Sometimes new members of a team are unable to accept the basic nature of the team culture and are disruptive or unproductive in the team structure. When this happens, it is best to remove them. This can often be done by allowing the rest of the team to bring so much pressure to bear on the misfit that he or she voluntarily leaves the team; however, the ultimate responsibility rests with the team leader.

The most effective medium for communicating important cultural values and beliefs is the establishment of jargon, metaphors, stories, and other types of rituals that are unique to a particular team. The members of a long-standing team at a large oil company seemed to communicate with each other in a cryptic and shorthand way, and an outside observer listening to them would have little idea of what was going on. But the team was able to progress through problem solving and decision making at a very rapid pace. In fact, this team had developed a series of buzz words and shared expressions that allowed them to cut down the amount of verbiage used in their communications and accomplish their tasks more efficiently.

## Role of the Team Leader in Shaping the Team Culture

Organizational cultures do not come into existence accidentally (Schein, 1985). Organizations are created by people, and the creators of organizations design organizational cultures by articulating their own assumptions and values. The essential function of a team leader is to manipulate the culture so that it becomes productive and efficient. To do this, a team leader must be constantly aware of what is going on in the team—the factors that promote team functioning as well as those that are dysfunctional. The leader must have the motivation and the skill to intervene in the culture and reshape it when that is desirable—to tear down the dysfunctional characteristics and reorganize the team into a productive structure. This takes a great deal of dedication and commitment. The leader must be able to absorb much of the frustration and anxiety that team members may experience while going through a change. For instance, when a member is dismissed from the team, the other members may experience a high level of anxiety; the team leader needs to deal with this anxiety head-on to reduce it as rapidly as possible.

The ability to change cultural assumptions is probably the most important function a team leader can perform. A manager must be able to examine the assumptions, beliefs, and values that are in operation and must have the practical knowledge required to reshape them. Team leaders should promote their own beliefs and values as their teams become more effective but must also be open to the ideas and perspectives of team members. For team members to be able to expound on their beliefs and values and then to see how those beliefs and values fit into the team culture is part of the learning process.

A team leader must have a vision of how a team should function and clearly transmit this vision to all members of the team. To create a vision of what the team would be like when functioning most effectively, the leader must analyze the actual behaviors within the team—the way team members function interpersonally and the team's processes and procedures. In a team that has developed a highly productive culture, team members express a high degree of loyalty and trust; they have confidence in each other, knowing that others will carry out their various functions. There are a highly supportive climate in which people are willing to jump in and help each other, an openness to change and innovation, and a sense of excitement about the way the team is functioning.

Team leaders carry the burden of responsibility for establishing the kind of culture that produces effective teamwork. Although the task of building an effective team culture is not easy, it is essential. Building effective teams is a basic requirement of becoming an effective manager.

# 14

## Taking Charge of
## Team Productivity

One question tends to rear its head at this point in a book like this: will the reader be stimulated to action as a result of the material that has been presented? This chapter has been designed as an impetus for action—to provide incentive to utilize this book's ideas and thereby improve team productivity.

The most obvious and compelling reason for a serious study of how teams work is the need to improve the productivity of teams in all organizations. This reason is so obvious that it is often overlooked, and managers may be inclined to ask, "Why should I do this?" or "What's in it for me?" The answer is simple: "What's good for the organization is good for you." A serious examination of teamwork can lead to valuable discoveries that can make the difference between a moderately productive and a highly productive group of people. Improved quality and increased output will be a direct result of the talents of team members being unleashed. Many organizations in other parts of the world have discovered how to unleash the dormant talent within their work forces; American organizations can do the same.

If improved output alone is not reason enough to begin looking at team productivity, managers might consider team productivity from the point of view of their own career development. The changing direction of American management requires that managers of the future be fully versed and qualified in all the functions of managing, including managing team productivity. The U.S. Department of Labor, in conjunction with the American Society for Training and Development, recently issued a report entitled *Workplace Basics: The Skills Employers Want* (Carnevale, Gainer, and Meltzer, 1989). According to the report, if the competitive position that American organizations have experienced in the past is to be maintained, managers and members of organizations must have not only a solid business education but also skills in the following essential areas: teamwork, oral communications, listening, learning how to learn, goal setting, motivation leadership, self-esteem, problem solving, creative thinking, personal and career development, and interpersonal negotiation.

Once a manager had realized the significance of learning how to improve team productivity, the next question is how to take charge and move ahead. Organization politics can often work against a manager who is attempting to assume responsibility for making needed changes. However, a manager can take action by discovering the positive ways of being political and entrepreneurial (Block, 1987). A manager can either maintain the status quo, remaining cautious and dependent on the organization, or be courageous and autonomous. The results of following one's entrepreneurial instincts honestly and affirmatively can be extremely beneficial for both the individual and the organization.

In the typical bureaucratic organization, politics tend to be destructive, forcing people to say things that they do not really believe, breeding suspicion and concealment, and causing issues to be dealt with in guarded and ineffective ways. If managers believe in the power of teams, they can take on the responsibility and authority for improving their own organization while encouraging the same type of action in people working around them. It is through a strong commitment to the idea that improved teamwork really can make a difference that a manager can exert a constructive form of organizational politics. In short, to make things change and to improve productivity in an organization, the manager should do the following:

1. Make a commitment to yourself to improve.
2. Be an architect of your own organization.

3.   Set goals that are unique and that others have not achieved.
4.   Choose the path of highest resistance rather than the one with the least resistance. The payoff will always be higher.
5.   Take some risks because it is the right thing to do and needs to be done.
6.   Recognize that you are an entity in yourself and that you can initiate change.
7.   Know that you are responsible for your own problems. What you have is what you have made.
8.   Do not wait for the signal from above. The ball is in your court, and you can throw it any time you wish.

Managers sometimes run into stagnation resulting from old habits and ideas that have become entrenched within an organization, and such stagnation can drag down innovative efforts at improvement. There are ways to circumvent such problems and resistance by taking advantage of the positive feelings and the desire to move ahead that are found in all organizations. People do look forward, and they do want to improve and win; when changes are linked to these human desires, positive responses and results will follow. A second problem commonly encountered when change is undertaken is insufficient time to make the change. Managers are often so caught up in day-to-day fire fighting that they never set aside the time to work on general improvements in areas such as problem solving. Time must be spent working on projects that will lead to improvement, not just on keeping the organization from slipping below its present level. Although this extra time is difficult to find and sometimes painful to spare, it is very productive time.

As managers start to change the way they manage their groups, they often find a clear and pronounced drop in productivity. Every effort at change entails a learning process, and it is during this learning process, this transition period, that productivity temporarily drops. Be assured, however, that the drop will be followed by an increase in productivity that will surpass the previous level. Managers also frequently encounter resistance. The solution is not to try to clash directly with those who resist but to work around them. Find ways to work with those who are receptive and enthusiastic and simply avoid those who are resistant. In time, those who resist may see the light and come around to your position. Finally, managers attempting to initiate change may experience the feeling of a loss of power. Managers have been taught over the years to feel powerful and to strive for power within their organizations. A manager who delegates power or responsibilities to members of the team may feel that he or she is giving up something important. In reality, however, the manager is not giving up power but simply sharing it with other people. The manager will still be held accountable and will in fact be seen as more powerful for having made the team more productive.

Managers can do a number of things to initiate change on their own. First of all, they can develop their own vision of how they see the organization working, commit this vision to writing, and then share it with members of the team. The vision serves as a picture or target that people can easily identify with, and it can stimulate them in a similar direction. The second thing managers can do is start changing their own styles of managing. This can be done by simply introducing new behaviors and actions, one at a time, watching the results of these actions and behaviors, and then making them a part of a permanent leadership approach. Third, managers can seek out support from members of the team who are interested in a more team-oriented approach. Peers can also serve as a source of support, information, and ideas that assist managers in implementing a team-oriented approach to managing. Fourth, a manager can experiment with specific areas in the way the team works. For instance, problems such as poor team meetings can be addressed directly with the team. Team members will view this as improvement and moving ahead. After one or two successes, the whole process of changing the team will begin to unfold. Finally, managers can observe other successful teams, read about self-directed teams and team productivity, and attend seminars and workshops on the subject. The following steps are suggested as an agenda for action:

1.  Start by preparing a vision of how you see your team working two or three years from now. Discuss this with your team members, visualize it with them, and gain their commitment to reaching it.
2.  Study and understand your team members. What are they like? What do they need? What do they want? What can they contribute to the team? How can you set up a culture that will tap their unused and unleashed resources? Work with them in this process.
3.  Analyze the way your team is working today. Use a survey or whatever method is best suited to your needs to help you diagnose and understand the team problems that you are now experiencing. Share these problems with your team. Get them to help you develop action steps to correct the problems.
4.  If needed, enlist the help of outside resources. Most organizations have their own specialists who are qualified to assist as facilitators and team builders. If there are no such specialists or resources within the organization, go outside.
5.  Once a team has started to make the change, be sure that you have designed ways to monitor the improvements. Provide ways to reinforce the change in a positive way, and reward the team for the successful adoption of action steps that increase its productivity. The improved results will themselves be rewarding, but it is helpful to offer more tangible rewards as well: special recognition, favors, opportunities for personal development, financial rewards. If possible, try to design your system so that the more people produce, the greater the financial reward.

The whole issue of managing productive teams boils down to what is in it for you, the team leader. When you get improved performance from your team, you will feel greater satisfaction with yourself, your work will be more fun, your career position will improve, and you will be on the way to greater financial reward.

# Appendix
# Additional Resources on Effective
# Team Management

Clearly, a single book cannot cover every specific detail of effective team management. This book has highlighted the most pertinent aspects of the subject to give managers an idea of its breadth and importance. There is a wealth of information and resources that have not been included. This Appendix provides a list of the most important writings on the topic of effective team management and several organizational sources of further help and information.

## Literature on Effective Team Building

### General Works

Baker, H. K. "The Hows and Whys of Team-Building." *Personnel Journal*, 1979, *58* (6), 367–370.

Berne, E.M.D. *The Structure and Dynamics of Organizations and Groups*. New York: Ballantine Books, 1963.

Bradford, L. P. (ed.) *Group Development*. (2d ed.) San Diego, Calif.: University Associates, 1978.

Dyer, W. G. *Team Building: Issues and Alternatives*. Reading, Mass.: Addison-Wesley, 1987.

Ends, E. J., and Page, C. W. *Organizational Team Building*. Lanham, Md.: University Press of America, 1984.

Francis, D., and Young, D. *Improving Work Groups: A Practical Manual for Team Building.* San Diego, Calif.: University Associates, 1979.

Jewell, L. N., and Reitz, H. J. *Group Effectiveness in Organizations.* Glenview, Ill.: Scott, Foresman, 1981.

Johnson, J. A. *Group Therapy: A Practical Approach.* New York: McGraw-Hill, 1963.

Klein, A. F. *Effective Groupwork.* Chicago, Ill.: Association Press, 1972.

Lorsch, J. W., and Lawrence, P. R. (eds.). *Managing Group and Intergroup Relations.* Homewood, Ill.: Dorsey Press, 1972.

Luft, J. *Group Processes: An Introduction to Group Dynamics.* (3rd ed.) Palo Alto, Calif.: Mayfield, 1984.

Merry, U., and Allerhand, M. E. *Developing Teams and Organizations.* Reading, Mass.: Addison-Wesley, 1977.

Miles, M. B. *Learning to Work in Groups.* (2d ed.) New York: Teachers College Press, 1981.

Mills, T. M. "Changing Paradigms for Studying Human Groups." *Journal of Applied Behavioral Science,* 1979, *15* (3), 407.

Patten, T. H., Jr. *Organizational Development Through Teambuilding.* New York: Wiley, 1981.

Scherer, J. J. "Can Team-Building Increase Productivity? Or How Can Something That Feels So Good Not Be Worthwhile?" *Group and Organizational Studies,* 1979, *4* (3), 335.

Tubbs, S. L. *A Systems Approach to Small Group Interaction.* New York: Random House, 1988.

Varney, G. H. *Teambuilding: A Self-Directed Approach to Improving Work Teams.* Bowling Green, Ohio: Management Advisory Associates, 1985.

Woodcock, M., and Francis, D. *Organisation Development Through Teambuilding.* Aldershot, England: Gower, 1981.

Zenger, J. J., and Miller, D. E. "Building Effective Teams." *Personnel,* 1974, *51* (2), 20–29.

### Assessment of Teams

Demeuse, K. P., and Liebowitz, S. J. "An Empirical Analysis of Team-Building Research." *Group and Organizational Skills,* 1981, *6* (3), 357–378.

Guetzkow, H., and Dill, W. R. "Factors in the Organizational Development of Task Oriented Groups." *Sociometry,* 1957, *20* (3), 175.

McConnell, T. *Group Leadership for Self-Realization.* New York: Petrocelli Books, 1974.

Moore, M. L. "Assess Organizational Planning and Teamwork." *Journal of Applied Behavioral Science,* 1978, *14* (4), 479.

Sherwood, J. J., and Woodman, R. W. "Effects of Team Development Intervention: A Field Experiment." *Journal of Applied Behavioral Science,* 1980, *16* (2), 221–227.

## Conflict

Cole, D. W. *Conflict Resolution Technology.* Cleveland, Ohio: Organization Development Institute, 1983.

Smith, K. K. *Groups in Conflict: Prisons in Disguise.* Dubuque, Iowa: Kendall-Hunt, 1982.

Walton, R. E. *Managing Conflict: Interpersonal Dialogue and Third-Party Roles.* (2d ed.) Reading, Mass.: Addison-Wesley, 1987.

## Problem Solving and Decision Making

Boss, R. W. "It Doesn't Matter If You Win or Lose, Unless You're Losing: Organization Change in a Law Enforcement Agency." *Journal of Applied Behavioral Science,* 1979, *15* (2), 198.

Koprowski, E. J. "Improving Organization Effectiveness Through Action Research Teams." *Training and Development Journal,* 1972, *26* (6), 26–40.

Patton, B. R., and Giffin, K. *Problem-Solving Group Interaction.* New York: Harper & Row, 1973.

## Interpersonal Processes

Dailey, R. C. "The Effects of Cohesiveness and Collaboration on Work Groups: A Theoretical Model." *Group and Organizational Skills,* 1977, *2* (4), 461–469.

Kiesler, S. B. *Interpersonal Processes in Groups and Organizations.* Arlington Heights, Ill.: AHM, 1978.

*Team Leadership*

Boss, R. W. "The Effects of Leader Absence on a Confronta-
tion Team-Building Design." *Journal of Applied Behavioral
Science,* 1978, *14* (4), 469.
Goldstein, L. D. "Managers, Values and OD." *Group and
Organizational Skills,* 1983, *8* (2), 203–220.

## Other Sources

Sources of information and assistance within the organization include the training department in the plant or operation and managers with high performance records and good team skills. Consultants, both internal and external, can also help managers with team-management problems. Consultants who assist managers in team building can be located through organizations such as the following:

> International Registry of Organization
> Development Professionals
> 6501 Wilsonmills Road, Suite K
> Cleveland, Ohio 44143

> OD Network
> P.O. Box 69329
> Portland, Oreg. 97201

The following organizations sponsor regular team-building seminars:

> University Associates
> 8517 Production Avenue
> P.O. Box 26240
> San Diego, Calif. 92126

> NTL Institute
> P.O. Box 9155 Rosslyn Station
> Arlington, Va. 22209

# References

Argyris, C. *Management and Organizational Development.* New York: McGraw-Hill, 1971.

Berelson, B., and Steiner, G. *Human Behavior: An Inventory of Scientific Findings.* San Diego, Calif.: Harcourt Brace Jovanovich, 1964

Block, P. *The Empowered Manager: Positive Political Skills at Work.* San Francisco: Jossey-Bass, 1987.

Carnevale, A., Gainer, L., and Meltzer, A. *Workplace Basics: The Skills Employers Want.* Washington, D.C.: American Society for Training and Development and U.S. Department of Labor, 1989.

Chemers, M. M., and Fiedler, F. E. *Leadership and Effective Management.* Glenview, Ill.: Scott, Foresman, 1974.

Dyer, W. *Team Building: Issues and Alternatives.* Reading, Mass.: Addison-Wesley, 1987.

Francis, D., and Young, D. *Improving Work Groups: A Practical Manual for Team Building.* San Diego, Calif.: University Associates, 1979.

French, W. L., Jr., and Bell, C. H., Jr. *Organization Development: Behavioral Science Interventions for Organization Improvement.* (3rd ed.) Englewood Cliffs, N.J.: Prentice-Hall, 1984.

French, W. L., Jr., and Hollmann, R. "Management by Objectives: The Team Approach." *California Management Review,* 1973, *17* (3), 13–22.

Hill, R. Unpublished paper, ORION International, Ann Arbor, Mich., 1982.

Jewell, L. N., and Reitz, H. J. *Group Effectiveness in Organizations.* Glenview, Ill.: Scott, Foresman, 1981.

Kolb, D., Rubin, I., and McIntyre, J. *Organizational Psychology: An Experiential Approach to Organizational Behavior.* Englewood Cliffs, N.J.: Prentice-Hall, 1984.

Lawless, D. *Effective Management.* Englewood Cliffs, N.J.: Prentice-Hall, 1972.

Likert, R. *New Patterns of Management.* New York: McGraw-Hill, 1961.

Lippitt, G. "Group Development." In L. Bradford (ed.), *Improving Decision-Making with Groups.* (2d ed.) San Diego, Calif.: University Associates, 1978.

Lorsch, J. W., and Lawrence, P. R. (eds.) *Managing Group and Intergroup Relations.* Homewood, Ill.: Dorsey Press, 1972.

McClelland, D., and Winter, D. G. *Motivating Economic Achievement.* New York: Free Press, 1971.

McGregor, D. *The Human Side of Enterprise.* New York: McGraw-Hill, 1985.

Mayo, E. *The Social Problems of an Industrial Civilization.* Cambridge, Mass.: Harvard University Press, 1945.

Ott, J. *The Organizational Culture Perspective.* Homewood, Ill.: Dorsey Press, 1989.

Rubin, I., Fry, R., and Plovich, M. *Managing Human Resources in Health Organizations.* Reston, Va.: Reston Books, 1978.

Schein, E. H. *Organizational Culture and Leadership: A Dynamic View.* San Francisco: Jossey-Bass, 1985.

Stepsis, J. *The 1974 Annual Handbook for Group Facilitation.* San Diego, Calif.: University Associates, 1974.

Townsend, R. *Up the Organization.* New York: Knopf, 1970.

# Index